RESUME DNA
SUCCEEDING IN SPITE OF YOURSELF

JOHN SINGER

Resume DNA: Succeeding in Spite of Yourself

Copyright © 2016 John Singer. All rights reserved. No part of this book may be reproduced or retransmitted in any form or by any means without the written permission of the publisher.

Published by Wheatmark®
1760 East River Road, Suite 145
Tucson, Arizona 85718 USA
www.wheatmark.com

ISBN: 978-1-62787-384-0 (paperback)
ISBN: 978-1-62787-385-7 (hardcover)
ISBN: 978-1-62787-386-4 (ebook)
LCCN: 2016931176

*This book is lovingly dedicated to my wife, Sharon,
and our extraordinary DNA:
Caitlin, Zachary, Jordan, Jessica, and Matthew*

CONTENTS

Preface vii
Acknowledgments xi

CHAPTER 1 There's a Red-Light District in Every Industry . . . 1

CHAPTER 2 Road Trip! 7

CHAPTER 3 Extra! Extra! Read All About It! 13

CHAPTER 4 SARie, SARie Night (Developing Your SAR) . . . 21

CHAPTER 5 So, What Have You Done for Me Lately?
(Applying the SAR) 27

CHAPTER 6 Your Resume—Inspired by Actual Events 33

CHAPTER 7 Proof or Consequences 51

CHAPTER 8 Mary Kay Gets a Makeover 57

CHAPTER 9 But Wait, There's More!
(Your Sixty-Second Commercial) 69

CHAPTER 10 Does This Resume Make Me Look Too Fat?
(Throwing Your Hat into the Ring) 77

CHAPTER 11 There's No Business Like Show Business! 83

CHAPTER 12 Well Played, Sir! (Negotiations) 97

CHAPTER 13 The Art of the Spiel 107

CHAPTER 14 Networking Saves Lives 115

CHAPTER 15 Never, Never, Never Give Up 129

About the Author 137

PREFACE

I have a rather eclectic career history. I studied communications at the University of Arizona and moved out to Los Angeles to study business and creative writing at UCLA. I pursued my creative side working the graveyard shift at a Santa Monica radio station and performing stand-up comedy at The Comedy Store and the Improv for six years. I also wrote speculative comedy scripts for television and actually received money for a script that I wrote for a Disney television show (that never aired). Hmm, if any of my four children lived like this, I'd disown them. Wait, two of my kids are chipping away in the entertainment industry as I write this—never mind. I then moved back to Oklahoma to start a family and enter the oil business.

As always, my timing was impeccable; oil was eighteen dollars a barrel, and the industry was experiencing a horrible recession. Oil tycoons were either jumping off the rooftop of the Petroleum Club (a one-story building) or sleeping on a park bench, pleading, "Please, Lord, give me one more chance and I promise not to screw it up again!" The oil business suffered for several more years, but all along the way, I was fortunate to learn valuable business lessons from my father at the best time: when business is at its worst. I later built and operated three radio stations and for the first time experienced the business side of radio. After selling the stations, I moved my growing family to Arizona and entered the outplacement industry.

Now, how does my patchwork past qualify me to coach others and motivate professionals to secure their next position? For over a decade (if you're doing the math, I'm ninety-seven years old), I have worked with thousands of clients individually and in group workshops, coaching them on the best way to showcase their skills, education, and expertise. I have taught professionals how to best use and expand their existing networks and to control an interview by providing information that is needed to receive an offer. I have written thousands of professional resumes, determined to customize the documents to where each is as unique as a snowflake. What makes resume writing fascinating to me? Summing it up into one concept: Defining the inimitable information that distinguishes one person from all others. I call this "Resume DNA."

In today's competitive job market, we need marketing collateral and specialized tools to set us apart from the competition. A strong resume is critical. How do you create and organize the pertinent data that is required to distinguish you from others who may be equally or even more qualified than you? It's a buyer's market in an employee's emporium. Are you discounting the "product" (you) or designing proper product placement? Many applicants don't realize that they repeatedly discount themselves by formulating their resumes with basic information that they have seen others use. They run the risk of blending into the masses, never being noticed or seen.

Today, small, medium, and certainly large companies use various forms of Applicant Tracking Systems (ATS) to manage resumes and applicant information. Job-search sites (CareerBuilder, Monster, LinkedIn, HotJobs, etc.) use ATS programs to manage the data from millions of resumes and deliver a group of "qualified candidates" to the companies that post positions on their websites. Then the list of candidates is whittled down further through the company's HR software. If you are fortunate enough to get past the initial ATS scan of key words and phrases and your precious document falls into the hands of a human resources director or hiring manager, what are the odds that you will make the cut for the initial screening? If an HR director has twenty resumes to review, they will only dedicate fifteen to twenty seconds to each resume before making a commitment to read on. Where will they be fifteen seconds into your resume?

The purpose of this book is to provide you with a better understanding of product placement—you are the product, and the companies and industries that you approach are the consumers. How do you address each consumer's needs? You have to define your hard skills, soft skills, professional experience, and accomplishments in order to accurately identify and brand yourself, the product. The ideas and methodology that I am presenting are offered with one simple goal: to teach you how to write a winning resume and develop an interview and negotiation technique that will provide key information leading to an offer.

There are no golden templates to provide a quick fix to where you can easily paste generic information on a page and push print. If there were such a magical process, I'd develop it into an app for your mobile device. It is your responsibility to develop the information that a prospective employer needs to hire you, and in doing this, you will also cultivate a professional strategy for securing your next position.

With all of the mystery and science that surround modern resume writing, just remember one thing: the only purpose of a resume is to entice an interview. No one can produce an accurate document without the basic ingredients that make you *you*. Ignore the man behind the curtain—you had it within you all along.

ACKNOWLEDGMENTS

Special thanks to David Finer, Avrom Greenberg, and Dexter Williams for your valued friendship and support. My thanks and appreciation to Don Dingwall, Stacy Malsom, Christine Bourne, Bill Jeffries, Susie Briggs, AJ Jimenez, Todd Singer, Melodye and Mark Fitch, Chris Laughter, and Susan Howington for their inspiration and encouragement.

My love and gratitude to my parents, Herman and Helene Singer, who motivated me to passionately pursue my dreams and never give up—always reminding me that life is short ... and so am I.

CHAPTER 1

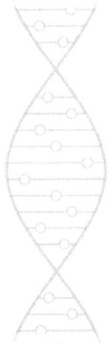

THERE'S A RED-LIGHT DISTRICT IN EVERY INDUSTRY

We formed our company, Professional Development Strategies, to move the outplacement industry in a new direction. We had been in the career-development industry for years and worked with hundreds of clients individually, coaching them on the best way to showcase their skills, education, and expertise, and teaching them how to best utilize and expand their existing networks. We have always loved our job of helping others.

Have you ever had a great job in a bad neighborhood? We were surrounded by similar organizations that guaranteed employment and were only interested in charging exorbitant fees. They rapidly moved prospects through an automated process that did not give them the tools necessary for lifetime career maintenance.

These questionable professionals promised positions. Anyone who promises that they will get you a job (for any amount of money) is lying to you. Anyone who promises that they will write a winning resume that will secure your next position is lying to you as well—and if you believe in their promises, you are lying to yourself. We've all seen the companies who offer career solutions for a hefty fee. Many of these career "specialists" may look familiar to you—they may have sold you your last vehicle or that time-share you overpaid for that is an albatross around your neck.

There are many companies who prey upon your desperation for a new position. They use antiquated methods to quickly develop your marketing collateral and blast your resume to the hallowed walls of Fortune 1000 companies (or any company in their database) in the hope that one resume will stick. It's the ol' "spray and pray" tactic: these companies actually prey upon you, spray your resume (leaving an unprofessional impression of you), and leave you to pray silently on your own. If you were in a position to hire a candidate and you received hundreds of emails daily through these "career partners," would you open a single document or direct these annoying spam packages to your trash?

Many people pay thousands of dollars for this "career service" and rarely see a return on their investment. At our company, we had one goal in mind when we opened our doors: to raise the bar on the delivery of outplacement services. Our group provides outplacement services for companies who have downsized and choose to offer outplacement care packages for their displaced employees. The company is providing the service, and the employee is receiving a valuable gift. Unfortunately, scores of professionals do not receive this service, so we also offer programs that coach these individuals. Many professionals have strong desires to move up, rather than out of their organizations. We put both groups through the same process: we help each client build a customized resume, develop interview and negotiation skills, and—most important—learn effective networking methodology.

There are bad companies in every industry. Before you invest in a partner to assist with your job search, do your homework. Once you are armed with the proper tools to launch your search, and realize that only you are responsible for your success, be prepared to make this your full-time job.

I recall one particular client who had gone through our program and possessed all of the necessary tools to start his job search. He was a self-proclaimed procrastinator, and in one of our coaching sessions, he started to break down emotionally. He admitted that he was not applying himself in his job search. He had been unemployed for three months; the wolves were at the door, and he felt paralyzed. He spent his entire day robotically applying for positions online and was admittedly exhausted from what he metaphorically referred to as "treading water in the middle of the ocean."

I asked him if I could join him for a moment in the big blue sea. His expression shifted to a confused look (much like yours at this moment), and I told him that I wanted to be right there by his side. How's the water? Is the sun shining? (Don't worry—this is not a "Footprints in the Sand" analogy.) He started to play along, and he asked me if I had brought sunscreen. I told him that there might be more than just choppy waters on our horizon. I bothered to look in all directions and spotted a small sandy island about two kilometers away. Why don't we use the same energy and determination that we are expending to keep our heads above water to instead *swim* toward our target?

You must establish your brand and envision a target. If you are persistent and completely engaged, you will be successful. Also understand that a proactive, self-managed job search is not an overnight process. If you expect others to secure a position for you, are you also expecting them to assume the daily responsibilities of your new job as well?

Only you can make this happen. To quote Robert Frost, "The best way out is always through." Let's start this journey; let's identify your Resume DNA.

CHAPTER 2

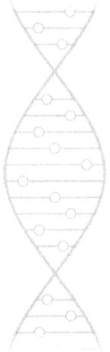

ROAD TRIP!

Before you start your professional journey, you must develop a plan. Your plans may change frequently, but you need to chart a course before you take your first step. I have been creating ten-year career maps with clients for over a decade. It would be interesting to see how many of the maps we penned ten years ago remained on course. I'm sure that very few stayed on the interstate—I'm quite happy with that assumption. How many of us have predicted our own futures in love, family, work, and health and not experienced unexpected twists and turns?

I started with a plan, but my career compass could double as a refrigerator magnet; it's been all over the place. While my compass has spun in erratic and unpredictable directions, I have remained flexible, recognized opportunity, and stayed on course to attain my ultimate goal. I still insist that we all must have a plan, and we can tweak it along the way. Let's look at a basic road map:

CAREER PATH

	Recent Position	Next Position	In Three Years	In Five Years	In Ten Years
COMPENSATION	$76,000	$80,000	$95,000	$120,000	$150,000
POSITION	Engineer	Project Manager (Engineering)	Program Manager/ Director (Engineering)	VP/Director of Operations	COO
INDUSTRY	Aerospace	Aerospace/ Manufacturing	Aerospace/ Manufacturing	Aerospace/ Manufacturing	Aerospace/ Manufacturing
LOCATION	Dallas	Dallas/ Houston	Open (Southwest)	Open (Southwest)	Open
EDUCATION	BS (Engineering)/ PMP	BS/PMP/ Completing MBA	BS/PMP/MBA	BS/PMP/MBA	BS/PMP/MBA

By establishing a ten-year goal, you can reverse engineer the map to see what your next logical step should be to attain that goal. At each step, the map will help you identify the Decision Maker (DM) you should be approaching for an informational exchange or job interview. A DM is the person one or two levels above your desired position. Most often it's a good idea to stay away from the person holding your targeted position; they may fear that you are after their job and could be intimidated by you. In the sample map above, the DM would be a COO, vice president, or director of operations. You now have an idea of who your audience will be as you prepare your marketing collateral.

As you develop the information on your skills and abilities, hard skills are an essential component of any resume. When you peruse the Internet for job opportunities, you probably enter specific industries or positions into the search bar. This is a good starting point, but you also need to use strategic keywords that include your certifications, level of education, and core competencies. These are your hard skills.

The following list of hard skills was developed by a client who was an Operations Manager:

HARD SKILLS

- Project Management
- Operations Management
- Business Plan Development
- Staff Recruitment
- Policies and Procedures
- Budget Development / Analysis
- P&L Analysis
- Budget Projection
- Labor Control Studies
- HR Management
- Procurement Planning
- General Accounting Skills
- Public Speaking
- Training Programs
- Sales / Cost Analysis
- Logistic Skills
- Team Building / Coaching Skills
- Word, Excel, PowerPoint

If this client enters any of the above hard skills into a search bar on a job board, she may uncover job postings seeking these specific skills.

When HR professionals review your information, they immediately zero in on your hard skills to determine if you are qualified for the position. Applicants should continuously conduct research to identify current market language and in-demand skills. By reviewing various online job descriptions for positions in your industry, you will have a clearer understanding of what the employer is seeking in an ideal candidate.

In the following job posting for an Operations Manager, the applicant underlined the company's key requirements:

> Responsible for developing and managing <u>annual research budget, productivity analysis, financial reporting</u>, and <u>analysis</u> for research administration. The candidate works with the institutional finance department to <u>develop</u> and disseminate <u>monthly research productivity financial reports</u> at the departmental, investigator, study, and organizational level. The candidate is also responsible for <u>developing business plans</u> for short-term and long-term goals and managing <u>purchasing and expense tracking processes</u>, utilizing internal controls and <u>reconciliation practices. Implements and communicates organizational mission, values, and divisional strategic plan</u>. Prepares, justifies, and administers <u>operating and capital budgets. Monitors financial performance</u> through <u>key metric analysis. Audits, monitors, and manages the charge capture and charge reconciliation processes for the site/clinics</u>.

The applicant possessed many of these desired skills but had not identified them in her original list of hard skills. After further investigation of the company and its management team, my client was determined to apply for the position. She would now need to polish her resume to include the desired skills and write a cover letter that clearly showed how she is perfect for the position.

As you start your professional self-analysis, you must identify and list your hard skills, soft skills, education, certifications, and depth of experience. These are essential when establishing your brand.

CHAPTER 3

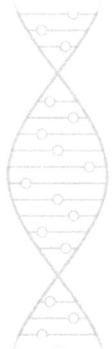

EXTRA! EXTRA! READ ALL ABOUT IT!

A few years ago, my son and daughter were on the front page of our local newspaper. There was no family scandal; the story was an inspirational piece showing how today's younger generation is taking a stand for what is right in our world by exhibiting their cause through creative expression (a theatrical production, in this case). Always the proud father, I shared this great joy with my immediate world. Friends and family were easily impressed. One notable felicitation remains fresh in my mind: "Fantastic! You must be so proud! Was it top fold?"

Thanks, Mom. That's another book: *My Brother Was an Only Child*.

A good point is brought up here. When we pass by the corner (now nearly extinct) newspaper coin box, we quickly gaze above the fold of the paper before determining whether we will invest in the product. What on your resume is grabbing the reader's attention when they look at your "top fold" for ten seconds? Fold your resume in half and be hard on yourself. What do you see? Do you see a brand, a summary of your areas of expertise, and one or two short stories about your major accomplishments? Probably not.

A resume has its own unique language. Your word processor will undoubtedly spray green lines throughout the document to alert you to suggested changes in your sentence structure. You are now writing in a specialized format that would make Shakespeare's quill spin. Here are a few basic rules to follow:

- ❑ Never use any pronouns to describe yourself.
- ❑ Numbers nine and under should be spelled out.
- ❑ Remain consistent throughout the document with formatting, fonts, and sizes.

Your resume should begin with an opening profile, a four to six-line summary of your qualifications that brands your level of professionalism and defines your key skill sets. The profile demonstrates *how* you get the job done, not *what* you do. I don't want to know *what* you do. I have five people in my lobby who do what you do. How are you going to solve my problems?

Why do I want to hire you?

- ❏ How do you make me look good?
- ❏ How do you make my company look good?
- ❏ How do you solve all of the problems that I tucked away in my drawer when you walked into my office?

In business, we all have problems during the best and worst of times. Part of a good interview strategy is showing where you add value—as a problem solver. This is where your stock goes up immediately.

Your profile is the first component of your resume and should lead off with a branding statement showing your level of professionalism. This is your first impression to the reader; the information that you lead with is crucial. Establishing a brand in the opening of the profile will immediately identify your level of professionalism and who you are as a professional. I'm reminded of a time when my mother was "branding" a potential beau for my sister: "He's a doctor! He's very handsome and tall … ish. He comes from a good family and went to Harvard! Did I mention that he's a doctor? Graduated at the top of his class!" Now, that's branding.

The hiring manager looking at your resume may have two hundred resumes to scan. Have you captured their attention with a dynamic branding statement that will encourage them to process additional information? The profile should also outline your soft skills and hard skills to show *how* you get the job done.

You should tailor your profile by using key words and phrases for each unique job opportunity. Be careful not to use clichéd, trite, or timeworn words to describe yourself. Be aware of modifiers that are current in your industry. How do you uncover such key words? They are usually revealed in the job posting. If the position requires "lean," "Six Sigma," "staff development / retention," or "onboarding" expertise, if you possess these skills, you need to promote them up front.

What type / level of professional are you? A branding statement like the following should be used to convey this information:

> An accomplished, dynamic management professional with over ten years of senior-level expertise in operations, finance, logistics, and new-business development.

Are you using key words and phrases that will pepper, power, and propel your profile, piquing the reader's interest for more information? The profile is the first cousin to the "TMAY." The TMAY is that awkward moment in the interview when you are asked to "**Tell me about yourself.**" When this request is made, you need to be able to present your unique skill set without delay.

The profile acts as a table of contents for the resume. When we think of a manager, we think of a person who manages both people and projects. In four to six sentences, you need to brand yourself, cover your people-management skills, and close with your project-management expertise.

Here several keywords that can be used in your profile to highlight your people-management skills:

lead	guide	motivate	direct
mentor	supervise	teach	train
promote	coach	collaborate	deliver
encourage	inspire		

When discussing your project or task-management experiences, consider using these keywords:

create	develop	evaluate	analyze
design	prioritize	build	launch
facilitate	implement	author	research
streamline	negotiate	coordinate	produce

How do you get the job done? Here is a profile using keywords (italicized for this example):

A *dynamic, self-motivated* professional with over fifteen years of senior-level management experience in operations, IT architecture, logistics, and new-business development. Applies a *mentoring* style of management by *guiding, training, coaching,* and *inspiring* associates to offer their own unique skills and talents and *collaborate* as a team to exceed the company's goals and objectives. *Creates, develops* and *implements* innovative programs that *streamline* daily operations and boost productivity and profits for the organization.

Your profile should brand you right off the bat. You should adjust your profile for every application and interview, highlighting the skills that are most valuable to that company and specific position. To feature additional skills, a section containing areas of expertise or core competencies is recommended:

AREAS OF EXPERTISE

- Global Logistics
- Conflict Negotiation
- Process Improvement
- Tactical Planning
- Top Secret Security Cearance
- Flight Line Management
- Performance Metrics
- Operations Management

When select skills are mentioned in the profile and highlighted in your areas of expertise, you are creating a "Table of Contents" of what the reader will be seeing throughout the rest your resume.

When it comes to talking about ourselves, most of us are ill at ease and uncomfortable. If we walked around talking about ourselves in everyday life, we wouldn't have many friends and probably wouldn't have a job. I believe that the job interview is the only venue, aside from politics, where you are expected to talk about yourself and share your greatest professional achievements. (Aren't politicians trying to secure a job as well?)

You are not bragging or boasting when you are communicating your education, skills, and achievements. Nobody else will do this on your behalf. You are sharing factual, pertinent information that supports the content in your resume and clearly separates you from your competition. But you have to be prepared to back this up.

I once had a challenging client who was overly impressed with himself. He constantly spoke of himself in the third person:

"At seventeen, I was recognized as one of the top one hundred most intelligent high school students in the United States. Lawrence is *always* the smartest person in *every* room."

"Well, Larry," I replied, "that might be true, but since there are only two of us in here—and my name isn't Lawrence—how do you think you just made me feel? When I was seventeen, I was still trying to master English as a first language."

His wife once told me that she overheard him making the same pitch in a phone interview. The interview ended abruptly, and her silver-tongued husband could not understand why. "Lawrence finds himself flummoxed."

Lawrence's external observation of himself revealed his profuse narcissism, which could be deadly in an interview. I worked with him extensively. I put him through several mock interviews and eliminated his arrogant third-person characterization of himself. It was much like *The Taming of the Shrew*, but Lawrence was a bright guy (as I was frequently reminded), and he finally got the idea—except for his written material. He rewrote the profile that I had created for him, leading with "A brilliant nuclear engineer with proven ability to solve impossible ..." I asked him to put himself in the shoes of hiring managers reading his resume. They would either be intimidated or amused (neither favorably) by this opening remark and would most likely cast him aside. I kept a watchful eye over all of his letters and resumes. I coached him before every interview. One evening I got a call:

"Lawrence got the job!" the voice on the phone excitedly articulated.

"Congratulations, Larry," I replied.

After you have customized your profile and areas of expertise, you will note your accomplishments in the next section of your resume. It is important that the skills (key words) that were featured in the previous sections are included within the stories of your achievements:

> **Designed** rehire criteria to comply with new state law that mandated rehires could not be reinstated solely by the use of seniority. Collaborated with stakeholders to identify the critical attributes needed by this particular employee group to be considered for rehire. RESULT: Successfully established the first criteria-based rehire process ever used by this organization.

> **Organized** efficient and effective internal procedures to prepare department for accurate and expedited reporting. Provided guidance and established timelines to meet monthly goals. RESULT: Improved customer service by eliminating inefficient procedures through the use of technology.

Your accomplishments are known as "functional information." You own these achievements just as you own your level of education, neither of which has an expiration date. This timeless information defines you and separates you from the competition. There may be twenty other applicants who have the exact education and work history as you. When you add your accomplishments to your resume, there will not be another applicant on the planet with the same information. This is your Resume DNA.

CHAPTER 4

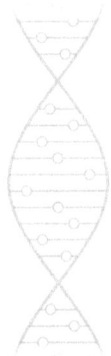

SARie, SARie NIGHT
(DEVELOPING YOUR SAR)

For the golfer: **PAR** (**p**roblem/**a**ction/**r**esult)
For the glamorous: **STAR** (**s**ituation/**t**ask/**a**ction/**r**esult)
For the rest of us: **SAR** (**s**ituation/**a**ction/**r**esult)

A three-sentence narrative (TSN) by any acronym is crucial. Whether you have created ten or fifty, TSNs are indispensable to your resume and mandatory inventory for your communication strategy. Part of your communication strategy is the way you position and share your accomplishments during an interview. This valuable information shows how you made or saved money for your previous employers or made significant contributions to those organizations.

When TSNs accompany your answers to interview questions, they put the proof in the pudding. A three-sentence narrative—a situation, your action, and the result—must be verbally communicated in one minute or less. As interesting as your achievements may be, you can lose your audience if you rant on and on. Most people talk too much in an interview because they are nervous and are not sure what needs to be said in order to move on to the next step. Don't dilute your message by watering it down with a superfluous explanation.

I compare this to a recent meeting that I had with a friend whom I hadn't seen for quite a while. As we chatted over coffee, he asked me how my kids were doing, and that opened up the floodgates. As I was wrapping up the rundown on child number four, I noticed a smile slowly exiting his face while his eyelids struggled to remain open. I felt like a hypnotist putting him under: "Your eyes are getting heavy. As I bore you with my children's accomplishments, you will become sleepy ..." Fortunately, I won him back by immediately asking about his kids, who, as it turns out, are slightly more accomplished than mine. Go figure. That was coffee with an old friend. In an interview, once you lose your audience, you'll never get them back.

If you control the interview by offering stories in the TSN format, you can cover six or more significant accomplishments as opposed to boring your interviewer(s) with two or three. First, communicate the situation (opportunity) and possible consequences of taking no action. Then briefly describe your action (what you did). And finally, state the *measurable* results of your actions. This narrative, called the SAR (situation/action/result), is an important part of controlling the actual interview.

But you first need to secure an interview through an interesting resume. My clients typically create thirty to fifty TSNs as I work with them to develop their marketing collateral. Your accomplishments, like your education, are eternal—there is no "best bought by:" date. If an accomplishment is noteworthy, it could have taken place at any time in your career. That is why you need to search your history extensively for notable achievements.

I have coached numerous clients with military backgrounds. Military clients have long histories of performance that are documented in their performance reports. For many, it is quite easy to look at their records and target dozens of significant accomplishments that will be ideal to showcase in their resumes. Other professionals need to take a hard look at their careers and write down accomplishments that are germane to the positions they wish to fill in the future.

With the key word and result bolded (for this example—not on the actual resume), here are a few TSN summaries:

> **Create:** Division needed immediate reorganization and revenue increase. Company planned to cut/downsize 23 department positions unless sales improved. Created and implemented a marketing and acquisition plan. **RESULT:** Increased sales and revenues by 20% and maintained staffing levels. Promoted to General Manager of Western Industrial Systems.

Organize: IT departments in various divisions and eight countries were unnecessarily duplicating projects. Organized an international IT management team to aggressively control costs. Applied cooperative teaming and project budget analysis to determine avoidable costs. **RESULT:** Executed plan and achieved an overall reduction of 17%.

Analyze: Recognized continuing loss of revenue in commercial loan department. Analyzed hundreds of commercial loans. Categorized loans throughout the United States, ranging in value from $100K to $20 million. **RESULT:** Assisted the company in reducing overall acquisition cost and increased ROI on portfolio bids ranging from $10 million to $50 million.

Look at your current resume and review your job history. Think back on the work you were doing in these previous positions. Hopefully, over the years you have assumed greater responsibilities and been promoted to higher levels. Why?

At your retirement dinner, as they are projecting an eight minute video tribute, encapsulating the last twenty years of your professional life – what accomplishments will the narrator be sharing with the tearful audience before they jump to their feet to give you a standing ovation?

Still drawing a blank? Talk with your family and coworkers, and you'll be surprised at what may surface. What was the initial problem or challenge? What did you do? What were the measurable results of your actions? We have each made a difference in some shape or form. Through our actions, we have not only improved a situation but have also left positive impressions on others.

As George Bailey rejoiced in *It's a Wonderful Life*, "Merry Christmas, movie house! ... Merry Christmas you wonderful old Building and Loan!" It has been a wonderful life, professionally. Share it with others.

CHAPTER 5

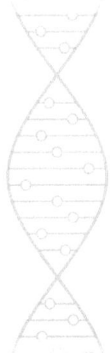

SO, WHAT HAVE YOU DONE FOR ME LATELY?
(APPLYING THE SAR)

After a client has secured a position, I advise them to take their "JAR" to work with them. I've received many a puzzled look. Jar of moonshine? Jar of marmalade? What is this "jar" you speak of? It's quite simple: you never stop recording your achievements. You have to maintain a **j**ournal of **a**ctions and **r**esults. This is the ongoing history of your SARs within the organization, and trust me, no one other than you will document this valuable information. Typically, you are going to be called in for an annual or semiannual review. The company may be on the verge of a massive downsizing: Who can we cut? Where is the fat in our organization?

In your review, you may not be discussing a raise or a promotion. Whether you know it or not, a good review may determine whether you will keep your job. You should be prepared both offensively and defensively. If you've been in the corporate world for any length of time, you've likely witnessed a top performer walking into a review with all the confidence in the world, only to exit the meeting with an empty box and a security escort. Our outplacement company has seen this happen repeatedly. The client comes to us in a state of shock: "I was blindsided. I never saw it coming! Just last month they were *praising* my performance!" "I can't believe this, after all I have done for them!"

This is a common tale, and the employer's decision to let you go cannot be reversed once the meeting is over. If your employer is aware of your accomplishments and the fact that they are better off keeping you, it may not save your job, but as my Grandma Rose used to say, "It couldn't hurt." In other words, be prepared to highlight your valuable contributions. Now, you need not live your life worrying that the ax is going to drop every six months, but you need to understand that this can happen at any time. No employee is irreplaceable or indispensable. If being let go is the worst-case scenario, how do you walk into a review for the best-case scenario? The same way, prepared.

I had a recent discussion with a young film editor in the entertainment industry. I use this as an example because some of our friends in Tinseltown don't believe that the common policies and principles governing the job market in the rest of the world apply to their industry. (So much for my movie deal.) The golden rule in Hollywood is "He who has the gold rules." The bottom line is, it's a buyer's market, and employers are in a unique position to hire and fire at will because there are hundreds waiting in line behind you to take your place.

David, the young editor, had a film degree from USC, a few small projects under his belt, and a burning desire to build a portfolio that would establish him in the business. He was brought into a small production company that produced interviews with celebrities for the Internet and television. David was initially a contractor, editing segments eight hours a day, five days a week. The company paid him a day rate of $150 and assured him that if he moved into a full-time role he would receive a daily rate of $200 with full benefits.

Happy to have work that would be a sizable building block for his resume, he gave the job his all. Within six months David was given a new segment to produce and edit, assigned a parking space, and congratulated for graduating to the full-time position. David was expected to work from 8:00 a.m. to 5:00 p.m. and be available around the clock for extra projects. Two of the five editors resigned to pursue other opportunities, and David's workload doubled. His supervisor told him that he would have to cover the additional projects. David's daily pay remained at $150 without health benefits, and he would have to be responsible for his own tax withholdings because he was still considered a 1099 contract employee.

Evidently, all of the editors were in the same 1099 boat. David was now working sixty hours a week, saddled with additional responsibilities and paid like an independent contractor. But a company cannot dictate your hours and responsibilities as if you were a full-time employee and consider you a 1099 contractor—this is illegal.

The company was not affiliated with a union, so it could compensate at lower rates—but this did not put the company above the law. David felt that if he blew the whistle with the Labor Department and asked for the pay increase that was promised earlier, he would be discharged immediately.

We advised him to be prepared at his upcoming review with a history of all he had contributed during his first six months with the company. David shared eight success stories (SARs) with his supervisor and reminded her that since he was responsible for his withholdings and health benefits, a $200 daily rate would be commensurate with his skill set and job responsibilities. He did not present this as a "my way or the highway" ultimatum—he just stated the facts. Since his employer was dictating his daily responsibilities and since he was working over forty hours a week at a fixed compensation, legally he should be designated a full-time employee with benefits.

David was called in for jury duty and notified his supervisor that he would be taking a few days off to perform his civic duty. When the jury duty ended (after only two days of absence), David's supervisor told him that no work was currently available and that his editing services were no longer needed. Interestingly, David saw a posting online from his company for his position. The company was clearly maneuvering around the law. There was a reason for the heavy turnover in film editors with this group; for years they just hired the next person in line when an employee addressed the company's standards, practices, and ethics.

When David applied for unemployment benefits, he provided clear evidence that he had been working full-time, but he was denied benefits due to his 1099 status with the company. An investigation was initiated into the company's business practices, and the company was heavily fined for breaking labor laws. This company had been abusing the system for years, and the fines were negligible compared to the thousands of dollars it had saved on unemployment contributions, withholding expenses, and benefits. Hooray for Hollywood.

We assisted David with his job search. The work he had done with the previous company was outstanding and enhanced his editing reel (portfolio) significantly. He now knew how to communicate his accomplishments by using SARs and how to clearly define and speak to any job responsibilities brought up in an interview. The same stories that fell upon deaf ears when pleading his case to his former employer were now applicable and appropriate for his interviews. By sharing his accomplishments, he could easily show where he could add value to an organization. With each offer that David received, he requested that the terms be put in writing, with the compensation, benefits, and—most importantly—the job responsibilities clearly defined.

David landed an editing position with a reputable company and negotiated a salary 50 percent higher than that of the previous position, along with an excellent benefits package. He accomplished this by communicating his strong skill set and showing where he could add value and solve existing challenges. He is on a successful path in a very competitive industry. Hooray for David.

Every situation is unique, and you must come to the table prepared.

CHAPTER 6

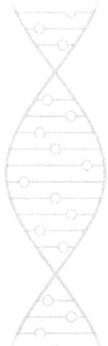

YOUR RESUME—
INSPIRED BY ACTUAL EVENTS

Your resume should not be "based on a true story" but it is "inspired by actual events." Your profile has defined your brand. Your core competencies have been identified through your soft skills and hard skills. You have documented your accomplishments with TSNs. You now have the ingredients to construct the functional portion of your resume. Functional information is essential when distinguishing yourself from others. When you apply online with the standard chronological information, you are easily grouped with candidates who possess similar job histories and educational backgrounds. A chronological format is just a basic snapshot of your work-history timeline.

When you infuse functional information into your chronological job history, you become totally unique—no two people share the same information. This is your Resume DNA. Some resume writers weave the subject's functional data within the bullet points under the listings for each position held. That is totally acceptable; at least the information is presented.

I prefer to write the functional information on the first page. By opening with a branding statement and continuing with TSNs, the client has one sheet that they can speak from in an interview. This is called a functional/chronological combination resume. Page one contains functional information, and page two is mostly chronological.

Accomplishments should always be written in a few sentences without the use of pronouns. We know you did this—it's your resume—so leave out the "I." The framework is simple: situation, action, result. You may wish to highlight the action words as shown in the examples below:

Transformed a small public-sector agency with a single focus to a dynamic and entrepreneurial entity. Implemented a strategy to give the agency the capability of pursuing multiple lines of business and develop new opportunities for economic growth for the community.

Modified the strategic direction of a small government defense contracting firm facing increased competition and decreased contract offers. Capitalized on the small size and agility of the firm, refocusing it toward business consulting and strategic planning, expediting the timeline to compete successfully for a lucrative municipal-government contract.

Refocused a multimillion-dollar social services agency from a traditional single-payer system to a multiline, fee-for-service business model. Diversified the client base and implemented a dynamic strategic communications plan that resulted in a wider donor base and increased revenue.

When your accomplishments are on the first page (and included in the "top fold") of your resume, the reader is immediately drawn to your achievements and may want to learn more. Don't bore them with how the watch is built; just tell them the time. In other words, a brief TSN can act as a foundation for discussions during an interview, and when asked to elaborate on the story, you can do so easily.

Following your list of accomplishments, you can anchor the first page with your education. Here is an example of page one:

RAYMOND KIRLAND
202-555-0237

www.linkedin.com/raykirland   ray.kirland@gmail.com

A dynamic, self-motivated professional with over fifteen years of executive management expertise in finance, operations, and new business development. Leads, trains, coaches, and inspires associates to utilize their own unique skills, creativity, and talents to collaborate as a team to achieve the company's goals and objectives. Creates, builds, and implements innovative systems that streamline the planning, organization, and execution of the operations, financial, and sales functions.

AREAS OF EXPERTISE

- Financial Analysis and Management
- Forecasting / Strategic Planning
- Team Leader / Builder
- Material Resource Planning
- Operations Management
- Warehousing / Distribution Management
- Budget Forecasting and Development
- Quality Control

PROVEN ACCOMPLISHMENTS

Analyze: Company sustained five straight years of losses and was facing imminent bankruptcy. The marketing budget equaled 25% of revenue, and losses were rising. Analyzed online advertising, created ROI break-even standards and recommended outsourcing of day-to-day marketing functions. Cut ad spending initially by 85%, and then gradually increased spending up to prior levels to recover sales. RESULT: Every sale created a profit immediately, resulting in a 10% annual profit.

Budget: Direct and overhead costs for manufacturing company were out of control, and profit was minimal to nonexistent. Created and implemented simplified line-item budgets and weekly variance reports for every department; trained and coached managers on the effective use of their budgets. RESULT: Production increased, costs were reduced, and inefficiencies were exposed, improving profits.

Motivate: Prior bonus plans raised expectations but failed to benefit employees, causing low morale and poor productivity. Profits and output dropped as labor costs dramatically increased. Developed and implemented a transparent bonus system, splitting any cost savings equally between the company and employees. RESULT: Production costs plummeted, and profits consistently exceeded budget expectations.

Planned: Construction projects were delivered consistently late and over budget. Management was attempting to control a process that they could only influence, not manage, adversely affecting profits. Created and implemented a weekly plan, placing the forecasting, implementation, and tracking responsibilities on the crews performing the work. RESULT: Allowing employees to create goals and perform to their own performance levels raised output and profits beyond management's expectations.

Collaborate: Multiple departments were entering design, product, cost, and pricing data into the ERP system, causing redundancies of effort, conflicting agendas, accounting discrepancies, and confusion for both employees and customers. Customer service calls, complaints, and invoice adjustments / refunds increased by over 300%. Collaborated with the department managers and IT to define each department's needs and obstacles. RESULT: Creating a single data entry window simplified data entry, literally putting all departments on the same page, which eliminated complaints, invoice adjustments, and accounting headaches.

EDUCATION
BA—Political Science—University of Arizona
MBA—Finance and Marketing—University of Arizona

How many pages should your resume have? Opinions vary. Some say one page is ideal, two pages are preferred, and three pages are too many. I believe it depends upon the level of the professional and the importance of the content being presented. When functional information is included, the resume should be at least two pages. When considering aesthetics, use a font that is easy to read. I recommend Arial, Calibri, or Verdana (sans serif) in a ten or eleven point font size. (Point size will vary with your font selection.) Many resumes are written in serif style using Times New Roman, Georgia, or Garamond. I feel that Arial (sans serif) is easiest on the eye.

There are dozens of fonts to choose from, but if you get too fancy, your resume will look "busy" and be difficult to read or process. If you were reading a book that was published entirely in **Comic Sans MS**, I doubt you would make it to the end. Stay away from heavy borders and cutesy graphics. Believe me, gimmicky formats are not appreciated and are quickly cast aside. Never insert your picture into a resume. If an employer wants to check you out, they can look you up on LinkedIn.

Always use a twenty-pound or twenty-four-pound paper. Cotton paper in this weight has the best feel, and when selecting a color, an ultralight gray or cream (ivory) looks best. White resume paper is acceptable but rarely stands out and usually gets lost in the shuffle.

Let's move on to the second page. This is where you will document your chronological job history. Do not open with an "objective". Employers know your objective is to work for them. Rather than to selfishly share what you want for yourself, why not *selflessly* provide what you can do for their organization? I never like to see the word *objective* appear in a resume:

Objective: To secure an executive level position with a progressive company in the technology industry.

Sure, pal, thank you for stating the obvious. I had no idea that you were seeking this executive level position with my company when you applied online for this executive level position with my company. Tell me, what was

President Eisenhower really like? How keen did the world look in black and white?

Instead, lead with a positioning statement that you wrote specifically for this company and opportunity:

> **Positioning Statement:** Utilizes analytical, resourceful problem-solving skills to support critical business strategies, consistently contributing to company-aligned goals.

The positioning statement should be tailored for the opportunity. Show the company what you can do for them over and beyond their expectations.

Your professional history (jobs) now follows in a chronological history, most recent to oldest. Whether we admit this or not, age discrimination is a fact of life. The tracking software or the HR screener will definitely note your age. Most of our clients are over forty, which is not ancient by any stretch of the imagination. I also work with professionals well over sixty-five who tell me they have over forty years of experience in their fields. Their interviewers are most likely under forty. If these older applicants instead state on their resumes that they have "over twenty years of experience" in their industries, they are still making a truthful statement without revealing their ages. (Isn't forty years greater than twenty?)

The goal is to get beyond the resume scan and meet with the interviewer face-to-face; at that point the interviewer can determine whether the applicant needs to be put out to pasture. With that in mind, I suggest going back ten to fifteen years on the chronological portion of the resume.

My client may object, telling me she was an executive vice president of IBM for global business development in Southeast Asia in 1988—aren't we going to mention that? Yes, but in a different component of the resume—and 1988 will never be noted. Immediately following the chronological work history will be a section covering *Additional Experience*. There, we will lead off with the IBM VP position and list others, but years will not be mentioned. We will capture her key accomplishments while on the job and move on to other information that will not reveal timelines.

When creating bullet points under each position title you have held, it is important to go beyond the simple tasks and responsibilities that the reader will assume you performed. You don't want to characterize your job history using the same requisites that are found online in the job posting for this position. It is better to show that you led, oversaw, supervised, or directed these basic functions and to provide functional examples showing successful outcomes. These will act as talking points during the interview. They will also reveal that you are a problem solver, capable of performing beyond the daily rudimentary job functions.

As mentioned earlier, successive to the job history is the section that lists additional experience. This section notes other positions you've held (prior to or concurrent with those listed above) along with any licenses or certifications you may have. You should also list volunteer work, community outreach, additional education, and bilingual or multilingual proficiency. This component reveals all of those interesting layers of you that have traditionally been difficult to place in a resume.

If I'm torn between you and another equally qualified candidate, whom do I choose? Probably the one who is most like me and fits within my company's culture. I don't want you to be a chameleon (Zelig) who attempts to be all things to all people. Always be truthful. But if there is a common connection, by all means, use it. That is why this section is fluid. You will want to insert interesting information that is relevant to each specific job opportunity.

As noted earlier, additional education and training should be inserted in this section. If you do not have a college degree but have completed some college coursework, mention the areas of study that are applicable to this job. It is not necessary to list your high school diploma—it is assumed that you have one. Those who have not secured their advanced degrees or who are in the process of completing them can mention additional education in this section of the resume.

The last section on the second page will lay out your technical qualifications. Most professionals know the basics—Word, Outlook, Excel, PowerPoint, QuickBooks—but if you don't write them down on your resume, employers may assume that somebody else performs these tasks for you. All of your basic and advanced technical qualifications should be documented.

Here is an example of page two:

RAYMOND KIRLAND
202-555-0237

www.linkedin.com/raykirland   ray.kirland@gmail.com

POSITIONING STATEMENT: Utilizes creative team building and strong leadership skills incorporating comprehensive skill set in finance, business process, and technology to conceive and implement profit-driven business strategies.

PROFESSIONAL EXPERIENCE

Black Tie, Inc.   Los Angeles, CA   2009–Present
Chief Operating Officer

- Led and managed company through fundamental changes in all departments, resulting in a successful turnaround and sustainable profits.
- Established and attained the profit goal. Changed processes and personnel as necessary to control marketing, product, warehousing, and distribution costs. Developed a strategic direction for the sales and marketing function, enabling the company to become the industry leader in online retailing of men's neckwear and accessories.
- Improved processes, changed behaviors, and provided the mentoring and feedback to managers necessary to attain their goals. Changed the company's previous online advertising method and mindset to one employing a controlled, aggressive, and profit-driven strategy.
- Overhauled the purchasing strategy and product pricing scheme by integrating a break-even calculator into the ERP system and established a minimum selling price for every SKU.
- Restructured the warehouse and distribution system to dramatically reduce product/material handling and manpower requirements.

Davis-Meyers, LLC   Dallas, TX   2000–2009
Chief Financial Officer/Chief Operating Officer

- Created a strategic plan and managed the plan to turn the company around and transform it into a production-oriented design and manufacturing firm. Managed the processes from design to prototype and testing to manufacturing and product sales.
- Grew the company by 400% over five years by narrowing the product and service offerings to better reflect the company's core competencies and manufacturing capabilities.
- Planned and maintained manufacturing schedules, which included labor, material, and equipment resources, to achieve throughput and cost-containment goals.
- Maintained quality-control standards and safety compliance. Developed new business and expanded the customer base.
- Developed a profit-driven pricing model for effective bidding. Maintained a bid/award ratio below 20%.
- Assigned the development of the weekly production schedule to the foremen, machinists, and finishers, which dramatically increased throughput and ROA, with near-zero defect rates.

ADDITIONAL EXPERIENCE

Owner/Operator (Environmental Enhancement, Inc.)—Victorian home restoration and specialty contractor • **General Manager** (Bolgos Dairy & Ice Cream)—Frozen-custard producer and wholesaler • **Operations Manager** (Kirland Auto Supply/Import Parts Warehouse)—Automotive Jobber/Warehouse, hi-performance and off-road store, machine shop • **Expertise:** SEO, SEM, Affiliate Marketing Management • **Volunteer Work:** Garfield County Housing Cooperative, Shriners Children's Hospital, Junior Achievement, Eller School of Management Community Service Program

TECHNICAL QUALIFICATIONS

Excel • Word • PowerPoint • Visio • QuickBooks Enterprise • Modified ERP and MRP Systems Adobe Acrobat • Dreamweaver

It is important to collect and organize your professional information before you construct the resume draft. Use the following resume-prep checklist:

RESUME PREP SHEET

EDUCATION INFORMATION:

Institution/Organization:	Country:
Program/Field of Study:	Degree Attained:
City:	Completion Date:
State/Province:	
Description:	
What courses, activities, and areas of interest did you enjoy the most?	

WHAT IS YOUR EQUIVALENT LEVEL OF EDUCATION?

No high school diploma	Associate's degree/certificate (approx. 2 years)
Vocational/technical training	Bachelor's degree (approx. 4 years)
High school diploma/GED	Master's degree (bachelor's plus approx. 2 years)
	Doctorate (master's plus 2–4 years)

EMPLOYMENT INFORMATION:

HOW MANY YEARS OF OVERALL WORK EXPERIENCE DO YOU HAVE?

1–5 years	11–15 years	21–25 years	31 years +
6–10 years	16–20 years	26–30 years	

SOFT SKILLS

The action words on the next page identify your soft skills. Your soft skills help you accomplish work-related tasks, but they differ from hard skills in that they are more related to your interpersonal skills, experience, and leadership capabilities. Create a list comprised of soft skills acquired from previous professional contributions or skills that are in current market demand. The list should include skills you use every day to accomplish tasks, manage people, and complete projects.

PEOPLE-MANAGEMENT ACTION WORDS

administered	analyzed	streamlined	produced
attained	chaired	consolidated	reviewed
contracted	coordinated	delegated	strengthened
developed	directed	evaluated	executed
advised	communicated	coordinated	recommended
improved	increased	coached	stimulated
led	launched	organized	supervised
encouraged	planned	prioritized	assigned
spearheaded	unified	reorganized	designed
clarified	familiarized	assessed	assisted
coached	counseled	delivered	referred
demonstrated	diagnosed	educated	guided
exhibited	expedited	facilitated	transformed
facilitated	guided	informed	persuaded
instructed	achieved	expanded	succeeded

PROJECT-MANAGEMENT ACTION WORDS

administered	allocated	collaborated	budgeted
approved	arranged	developed	compiled
classified	corresponded	drafted	programmed
computed	critiqued	exhibited	designed
conducted	converted	examined	executed
delivered	delivered	formulated	engineered
directed	diagnosed	identified	generated
implemented	evaluated	managed	inspected
interpreted	forecasted	negotiated	maintained
operated	innovated	purchased	organized
provided	investigated	reviewed	operated
researched	marketed	reconciled	prepared
resolved	organized	systemized	recruited
streamlined	planned	upgraded	repaired

Which of the words above best describe actions you've taken to get the job done? (Choose five to ten terms, and write them below. These can be used in your profile.)

PERSONAL SOFT SKILLS

STORIES OF ACCOMPLISHMENTS

For each identified action word (above), create a story (SAR) to describe how you affected change in a professional situation. Consider the following questions when creating each story:

- ❑ What was the *situation* or problem?
- ❑ What *action* did you take to resolve the situation or problem?
- ❑ What was the measurable *result* of your action?

Here is an example:

Analyze: Recognized continuing loss of revenue in the Commercial Loan Department. Analyzed hundreds of commercial loans. Categorized loans throughout the United States, ranging in value from $100K to $20 million. RESULT: Assisted the company in reducing overall acquisition cost and increasing ROI on portfolio bids ranging from $10 million to $50 million.

Create ten to twenty stories of your accomplishments, using the template below.

ACCOMPLISHMENT / FUNCTIONAL SOFT SKILL #1:

a. What was the situation or opportunity?

_____
_____

b. What was it costing the company? What were the consequences?

_____
_____
_____

c. What actions or solutions did you create or recommend?

_____

d. What were the results of your actions?

_____

ADDITIONAL SKILLS AND EXPERIENCE

What additional skills or experiences can you share? Include core competencies (budget analysis and forecasting, project management, team leader/builder, etc.), and identify your technical hard skills (QuickBooks, Adobe, Publisher, Excel, Access, PowerPoint, etc.) in the space below:

PROFESSIONAL EXPERIENCE
WRITING YOUR POSITIONING STATEMENT

A positioning statement replaces the "objective" section in the resume. The reader knows that you want to work for their company in a specific position—they have many other resumes in front of them stating the same obvious objective. You have more impact with a "positioning statement" that shows the unique skills and experience that you can bring to their company. Your positioning statement should be tailored for each individual opportunity. Here is a sample statement:

POSITIONING STATEMENT: Uses strong analytical skills and technical knowledge with an emphasis on customer requirements to produce quantitative and actionable results.

(Your) Positioning Statement:

Now that you have your positioning statement in front of you, focus on your professional past:

- ❏ Summarize your work experience into quick sound bites.
- ❏ Define what you believe to be the most important pieces of your professional history.

Extract from your professional history those parts that you believe most closely apply to your positioning statement. Move in descending order from your most recent position to your earliest. For each position held, you will create the components of a brief paragraph outlining what you were in charge of, what you were responsible for, and the tasks you conducted on a daily basis.

Keep your information brief and to the point. Write in terms of size, dollar figure, and numbers of people supervised. When no hard figure is available, write about the percentage of time saved and income saved or earned. Try to begin your sentences with your identified soft skills. This allows you to relay your unique leadership strengths and style to the reader.

USE THE EXAMPLE SHOWN HERE AS A GUIDE:

JOB TITLE	COMPANY	DATES EMPLOYED (YEAR TO YEAR)	LOCATION
VP Technical Relationship/ Project Management	Wells Fargo	2013–Present	San Francisco, CA

IN CHARGE OF:
Managing a portfolio of 25 projects for the Enterprise Data and Analytics Team.

RESPONSIBLE FOR:
Interpreting business requirements, ensuring the design will meet the customer's needs.

TASKS CONDUCTED ON A DAILY BASIS:
Ensure projects remain on track and on schedule.
Forecast time and costs for all project resources, without exceeding the approved budget.
Troubleshoot and resolve all project-related issues.

Functional/Chronological (Two-Page) Resume Example (next 2 pages).

ANNALISA KANE
415-555-0237

www.linkedin.com/annakane annalisakane@gmail.com

PROFILE: An accomplished, self-motivated senior-level professional with over ten years of management expertise in operations, IT, and finance. Creates, develops, and implements innovative programs to increase revenues and reduce expenses, providing customers with unique and relevant product and systems features. Exceeds company's expectations, delivering a professional and collaborative product experience.

CORE COMPETENCIES

- Project Management
- Budget Analysis/Forecasting
- New Business Development
- Operations Management
- Strategic Analysis and Planning
- Team Leader/Builder
- Excellent Presentation Skills
- Relationship Building and Retention
- Process Improvement
- Staff Training/Development

PROVEN ACCOMPLISHMENTS

Collaborate: Over 100,000 customers were reaching the end of their draw period and were contractually obligated to begin repayment of interest and principal. In most cases, customers would experience a doubling or tripling of their monthly payment, leading to an increase in collections activity. Collaborated with senior management and Systems, Legal, Compliance, Risk, and Customer Service Departments to establish payment plans that would be more beneficial to the customer and mitigate risk to the bank. RESULT: Bank saved millions of dollars by retaining the customers, reducing collections activity, and maintaining an on-time payment flow.

Implement: The Marketing Department was looking for an opportunity to launch a new line of credit features to customers in less than six months. Implemented a new interest-only payment option for bank customers to use. RESULT: Thousands of new accounts were opened, allowing customers to take advantage of the interest-only payment feature. The bank realized a significant increase in revenue and a strong retention of the customer base.

Create: The Home-Equity Project Management Office employed two separate project managers to oversee the business and technical aspects of all projects. Recognized the need to merge the positions in order to reduce expenses. Created a new project process called the Unified Delivery Model that would cross-train one project manager to function in both the business and technical roles. RESULT: Several projects were implemented successfully under the new model, with fewer customer issues reported. The bank realized $500,000 in savings, and productivity improved measurably.

Coach: A staff member, recently promoted to implementation consultant, was unsure of her abilities and lacked confidence with public presentations. Coached associate one-on-one to understand the process, recognize her abilities, and build her confidence for public speaking. RESULT: Within six months, her performance improved considerably. She is now regarded as one of the experts in the position and is frequently requested to participate in projects, delivering her presentations with great confidence.

Develop: A large bank merger created the opportunity for mainframe systems to be consolidated, allowing for accounts to be converted to the new system. Developed the requirements on how the accounts would be converted along with the designs, test plans, risk assessment, training, and implementation plans. RESULT: Several hundred thousand accounts were converted successfully, and millions of dollars in cost savings were realized due to the consolidation.

EDUCATION

BBA—Economics and International Business, New Mexico State University
MBA—Global Management, University of Phoenix

Annalisa Kane (continued)

POSITIONING STATEMENT: Uses a strong, comprehensive skill set in finance, analysis, process improvement, and technology to conceive and implement profit-driven strategies that positively impact all business functions.

PROFESSIONAL HISTORY

Wells Fargo — San Francisco, CA — 1997–Present

Vice President—Technical Relationship / Project Management (2013–Present)
- Manage a portfolio of 25 projects for the Enterprise Data and Analytics Team. The projects focus on initiatives put forth by our virtual channels teams.
- Ensure that the projects remain on track and on schedule.
- Forecast time and costs for all project resources, without exceeding the approved budget.
- Troubleshoot and resolve all project-related issues.
- Interpret business requirements, ensuring the design will meet the customer's needs.
- Collaborate with technology team to ensure that design is built properly and all goals are met.

Vice President / Project Manager 5 (2010–2013)
- Managed small, medium, and large projects on behalf of the Home Lending Project Management Group.
- Acted in a dual role as both technology and business project manager. Coached a team of four project managers and implementation consultants.
- Completed projects via the waterfall (SDLC) method, initiation to closure.
- Collaborated with project teams to draft all project artifacts, ensured the projects remained on track and on schedule, and worked with management on a weekly basis to report status.
- Successfully implemented systems changes for a large bank merger.

Assistant Vice President / Project Manager 4 (2009–2010)
- Oversaw the performance of a project manager and a business analyst to support servicing and global initiatives projects.
- Ensured that all projects remained on track and on schedule and worked with upper management on a weekly basis to report status.

Project Manager 3 (2006–2009)
- Managed projects of all sizes for Consumer Credit Group / Marketing Area through the entire SDLC.
- Collaborated with project teams to bring the project to a successful implementation.

ADDITIONAL EXPERIENCE

Payments and Statements Manager (Wells Fargo): Managed a staff of two business analysts and participated in all projects related to billing statements and payments for the Consumer Credit Group.
- **Operations Analyst (Wells Fargo):** Represented the Loan Servicing Team on all projects and communicated system changes to members of staff directly impacted by changes.
- **Certifications:** Six Sigma Green Belt • **Community Outreach:** American Red Cross, American Cancer Society, Habitat for Humanity, United Way • **Special Recognition:** National Sales and Service Conference

TECHNICAL QUALIFICATIONS

Microsoft Word • Visio • Excel • Outlook • Lync • PowerPoint • SharePoint • Microsoft Project Adobe • Shaw Mainframe • Hogan Mainframe • ClearQuest • Planview • IT Architecture

CHAPTER 7

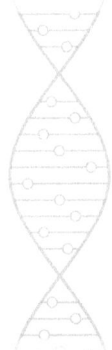

PROOF OR CONSEQUENCES

A client recently shared an email he had received from a competitor in his industry. The author of the email was attempting to position himself as an expert in their trade and belittle my client for his unique style of doing business. The email carried a negative tone and read as a stream-of-consciousness rant written in the late hours of the night with a bottle of scotch and a splash of venom.

It was quite obvious that the author did not proofread his document. The absence of punctuation and the six misspelled words did not compare to the closing statement: *"There is no room in our industry for people like you who insist on going rouge."*

Let's see—Dictionary.com defines *rouge* as:

rouge *n.*
A red powder, used as a cosmetic for adding redness to the cheeks.

A spellchecker will recognize *rouge* as a correctly spelled word—just as it will accept the spelling of the appropriate word: r-o-g-u-e.

When you unintentionally misuse or misspell a word, you appear to be uneducated, and your entire message loses any sense of credibility. As our poison-penned emailer may put it: "You're nothing but a scoundrel with rosy-red cheeks."

It is up to the writer to pay close attention to the content of their emails and letters. Words have many meanings. Read your messages out loud (we catch more mistakes that way), or have another person proof your work before you send your lyrical literature into the atmosphere.

I encourage my clients to send me the final draft of any letter, business plan, resume, or email before—I stress *before*—it is released. I want to be their second set of eyes, their final proofreader. I will usually find a mistake in their format or content. I work with highly educated and accomplished professionals—and many of them write like third graders. Why? Carelessness, mostly.

When a client sends a letter for me to review and tells me it was mailed yesterday, I'm wondering why they are wasting my time. I'm there to proof their work and maybe save them from embarrassment. I usually find several mistakes and will highlight their errors and send the document back for their wall of shame. Proofreading a document after it has been mailed is like closing the barn door after the horse has run away.

On many occasions, I work late into the night, reading letters and resumes out loud to catch any comma, *and*, *of*, or *the* that may be missing from the document. The cleaning crew in our building thinks I'm a little crazy when they catch me talking to myself alone in my office. Many times, I catch a sentence that doesn't make sense, has been repeated from an earlier paragraph, or has no reason to be in the document at all. Some people cut and paste carelessly and have the wrong person's name in the document, or they have carried over an inconsistent font, font size, or color. I read every word out loud because, for some reason, it is easier to catch our mistakes when we hear them.

Read your documents out loud. Have a friend or loved one read it as well. Then reread it two or three more times. Walk away from an email you have written and reread it an hour later; you may have a new thought or perspective to share before you finally push "send."

When a hiring manager reviews your cover letter and resume and sees inconsistencies, grammatical mistakes, or spelling errors, what kind of impression are you making? When you express that you are "detail oriented" in your profile and your resume is full of errors, do you think they will take you seriously?

If I see mistakes in a letter or resume, it tells me the writer simply does not care. If I were making the decision whether to select this person for an interview, I would disqualify them immediately. Check the documents that you currently have online with job boards, LinkedIn, and all of your social-media sites. There is a strong likelihood that you will find a mistake—hopefully it is not too embarrassing.

You only have one chance to make a first impression.

CHAPTER 8

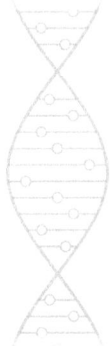

MARY KAY GETS A MAKEOVER

Recently I had a client who had completed the first phase of our ninety-day outplacement program. Mary Kay was an animated southern woman who jingled with every gesture. She dressed impeccably but was quite overstocked with her jewelry and perfume. Whenever she made a movement, her gold bracelets raucously reverberated like Santa's sleigh bells. Her delightful, overly applied fragrance lingered in my office hours after her departure. It was my job as her coach to diplomatically persuade her to reduce her perfume and jewelry by 95 percent. A little flustered by my suggestions, she fanned herself with her scarlet red fingertips and replied, "Well, I had no idea! I'll certainly follow your professional advice; you're entitled to your opinion. Bless your heart!" Being from Oklahoma, I know exactly what "Bless your heart!" means. It is applied as an antiseptic after a stinging remark: "He's as dumb as a bag of bricks. Bless his heart!"

I had already created Mary Kay's resume a few weeks earlier, and it was a darn good document, if I do say so myself. Mary Kay had started networking with industry managers and was well on her way to securing a position through several referrals. She spotted a position online that seemed to be a perfect match. On the career map we had prepared early in our process, she had designed a clear path in the manufacturing industry. Mary Kay's recent experience was in manufacturing, and earlier in her career, she had many years of experience in health care. The online posting was for a senior-level manager position in the health care industry. Mary Kay told me that the job was a perfect fit, and she had to apply. I told her that the first order of business was a resume makeover.

While some history in health care was mentioned in the original document, her resume was targeted toward manufacturing. We had to revise her profile to better brand her and rewrite her stories of accomplishment to focus on her achievements in health care as opposed to manufacturing. I teach clients modern resume writing techniques so they can be the custodians of their resumes for the rest of their careers. Mary Kay did an excellent job with her revisions, and with some additional polishing, her resume was ready for submission.

"Not so fast, Mary Kay. Now you have to write a conversational cover letter," I reminded her.

A little embarrassed, she sweetly asked, "Now, what was that again?"

"Weren't you paying attention in our map meeting three weeks ago? A conversational cover letter is your way of communicating how your skills, education, and experience perfectly match the company's key requirements as they are revealed in the job posting."

"Oh, yeah. The *letter*."

I went on to explain that with posted positions, she needed to create a cover letter that would show her fit with the company and expand on areas that her resume may not cover. I provided a sample letter and showed her the original job posting for which the letter was written. I pointed out how the client had clearly demonstrated how his skills, education, and experience matched the key requirements for the position. This is something that only you can do for yourself. No other person knows your background as well as you do. This type of cover letter allows you to use your own voice and tell your story effectively in a narrative style.

The conversational cover letter (CCL) should always bring up areas of expertise that your resume may miss. Here are two examples:

JONATHON HUNTER
214-555-4606

www.linkedin.com/jonlhunter   jon.l.hunter@gmail.com

October 12, 2016

Ms. Debra Ruiz
Director of Operations
Calico Engineering
11100 N. Oracle Road
Tucson, AZ 85739

Dear Ms. Ruiz,

I am writing to express my interest in the Senior Technical Manager position at your Tucson facility. As a seasoned leader with over fifteen years of experience in project management, I have the specific expertise and enthusiasm you seek to join your team.

    In my role as Project Manager / Project Leader for both Raytheon Missile Systems and Hughes Aircraft Company, I led several multifunctional teams in developing various missile assemblies and systems that successfully met the customer's goals. I have worked with both government and commercial customers and suppliers. I have created several successful proposals, leading multifunctional teams of 6 to 25 individuals with budgets from $5 million to over $300 million.

    I have developed presentations and briefed both upper management and customers. My mentoring style leads, trains, coaches, and motivates others to offer their own unique skills and collaborate as a team to achieve the company's goals and improve the organization. I believe that my 15 years of experience leading successful product-development projects will prove to be a tremendous asset to Calico Engineering.

    As a Department Manager for Hughes Aircraft Company, I led an organization of over 245 individuals in two locations (Canoga Park, CA, and Tucson, AZ), ensuring all projects were completed on time, independent of location. My varied experience has allowed me to master the ability to communicate with the broad spectrum of individuals and organizations required for successful operations management.

    In the final analysis, I am an experienced leader with developed organizational and leadership skills who possesses a strong passion for team building and developing organizations. If selected for this position, my commitment to you will be to work with your management team and staff toward taking the organization to greater heights.

    My resume is attached for your review, and I would welcome an opportunity to speak with you about the position.

    Thank you for your time and consideration.

Kindest regards,

Jonathon Hunter
Attachment

MATTHEW DELANY
555-555-0237

www.linkedin.com/mattdelany   matt.delany@gmail.com

January 11, 2016

Ms. Jessica Green
University of Arizona
888 N. Euclid Ave. #114
Tucson, AZ 85721-0158

Dear Ms. Green,

I note that your needs for the Director, Infrastructure Services position you are currently advertising coincide with my education, skills, and experience. Your posting particularly details the core requirements of my current position at Anderson Health Center, in which I have enjoyed significant success. Further, I am uniquely qualified for this position because I offer a background in project management leadership and oversight, IT infrastructure design and management, and strategic planning and execution.

During my professional career within IT, I have consistently been at the forefront of implementing change within my organizations, and I take pride in my ability to assist my customers in accepting and utilizing those changes. Throughout my career I have repeatedly experienced that you can accomplish more and guarantee a higher quality to the delivered product by working as a team than by working individually. I will bring to this position my extensive experience managing domestic and international strategic projects and providing leadership for multicultural, multifunctional local and virtual project teams.

Summarized below are projects that I have successfully completed at Anderson Health that specifically correlate with the "Duties and Responsibilities" specified within the position announcement:

- Built a cohesive and stable technical team within a department that had previously experienced excessive staff turnover
- Established strong relationships with multiple vendors, coordinating the delivery of all IT infrastructure services needed for the construction of a new 74,000-square-foot medical facility, on time and within budget
- Redesigned and implemented both the wide-area and local-area networks
- Re-engineered and upgraded the organization's phone system to a centralized, state-of-the-art VoIP telecommunications system
- Designed and migrated legacy server systems to a virtual server environment hosted on a modular enterprise blade platform

During my career, I have prided myself in being able to work effectively with executive staff by simplifying the technical concepts permeating the IT field and communicating with them in a manner devoid of technical jargon, while focusing on the basic costs and benefits of any proposal. I've also developed skills in working together with my organization's peers to implement changes and projects that improve productivity within the organization.

My education, skills, and experience will enable me to help address the challenges your program faces. I would like to arrange an interview to discuss the contribution I can make at the University Information Technology Services. I appreciate your time and consideration and will contact you to discuss the opportunity in the near future.

Regards,

Matthew Delany, MSM, PMP
Attachment

Back to Mary Kay. She came back with an excellent two-page letter, which I scaled down to a single page. Keep it brief and to the point. I advised her to submit her documents (resume and cover letter) online and also to print them on resume paper and send them via US Mail. Due diligence is necessary when writing a tailored cover letter; be sure to address it to a decision maker (DM) and include his or her title and complete mailing address. In the online submission, the cover letter should be addressed to the same person and formatted as if it were to be mailed on actual resume paper. When you are going the extra mile to write a customized letter, opening with "To Whom It May Concern" or "Dear Hiring Manager" diminishes the letter's impact. If you can't uncover the name and title of an upper-level DM, you can research the name of the HR director and use his or her name.

I then advised her to call the recipient of the mailed letter. She was resistant, saying she felt that the company frowned upon phone calls. I told her that there is nothing wrong with following up to see if the letter was received. The phone call is an opportunity to ask where the company is in its interviewing process and to make a third impression, which may elevate her above the competition.

I like to work in threes:

Impression 1: Polish your resume for the opportunity, and write a narrative conversational cover letter for the online submission. Most candidates merely push "submit," sending a generic resume without a cover letter. After Mary Kay submitted her documents, the applicant tracking software scanned the resume *and* letter for matching keywords. This was her first advantage.

Impression 2: Mail (don't email) your documents, printed on quality resume paper, to a targeted decision maker. This may allow Mary Kay to stand out and catch the eye of the DM, who may bring her in for an interview. In her letterhead, she included her LinkedIn address. Now the DM or HR director has an opportunity to investigate her further.

Impression 3: Make "The Follow-Up Call." If the employer penalizes you for professional persistence, this may not be a match made in heaven. You took the time and effort to stand above your competition and present a package that shows you are a perfect match for the posted position. Making a follow-up call to confirm the mailed documents were received and to ask where they are in the interview process at the very least puts you on their radar.

Mary Kay made her follow-up call a few days after her letter had been mailed and only made it to the recipient's gatekeeper. The conversation went like this:

"Donald Anderson's office. This is Debra. May I help you?"

"Hi, Debra. This is Mary Kay Bradford. Is Donald Anderson available?"

"Mr. Anderson is out of the office this week. Can I help you?"

"I'm calling to follow up on some correspondence that I recently sent to Mr. Anderson. I wanted to be sure that he received the documents."

"Yes, I saw your resume come through yesterday." The gatekeeper continued, "We are only reviewing online applications. Did you apply online?"

"Yes, I did. I also sent additional information for Mr. Anderson's review. If he has any questions, I'm available to discuss the materials with him. Can you please tell me where you are in the interviewing process?"

"If we are interested in your online application, we will contact you at the first of next week and start the interviews on the fourteenth."

"Thank you for your assistance. Please have Mr. Anderson return my call if he has any questions. Have a great day!"

"Uh huh ... you too." *Click.*

Now, that didn't go very well. At least Mary Kay made the effort, and her blip is slightly stronger on the radar screen. She made a third impression.

Well, as the story progresses, Mary Kay got a call from Debra the following week to schedule an interview. She called me immediately with the good news. I congratulated her and then told her not to get too excited. "Is this a phone interview where they are initially screening you? Is this an in-office interview with a lower-level HR manager?"

"It's an interview at their office with HR," Mary Kay replied.

"Well, it will probably be a screening interview to see if you are qualified to move forward. Now you have to spotlight your health care experience and let them know that you are up-to-date on recent changes in the industry. The interviewer will have to communicate that you are a qualified candidate to the powers that be. What have you done to prepare for this line of questioning?"

"Umm ..."

I prepped her with the proper opening statement, questions to anticipate, and questions to ask that would show how she brings added value to the position. Then I conducted a brutal mock interview. I felt she was ready.

The interview went well. A few days later, Mary Kay excitedly informed me that she was invited back for another interview.

"Congratulations! Don't get too excited. Who is the interview with?"

"It's a panel interview. I'm meeting with the CEO, Donald Anderson; the CFO; the director of IT; the marketing director; and the head of HR."

I informed her that she should do her homework on all of the panel participants. Be prepared for their questions. How will you work with each department? You may be their boss, if hired, but they are going to rake you over the coals during this interview. Check them out on LinkedIn, and send each of them an invitation to connect. We prepped for the interview with a role-play of anticipated questions and a list of questions for each of the panel members. She prepared drafts of thank-you letters, one for each panel member, filling in the blanks after the interview, and she mailed the letters the same day as the final interview.

Mary Kay received an offer, and I assisted her with the negotiation, during which she brought up additional value that she would provide. The final contract exceeded the original offer. I told her she could get excited now. Bless her heart.

What most impresses me about this story? I'm not surprised that she received an offer; she positioned herself perfectly throughout the interview process, and I was very confident that she would get the job. What impresses me most is that she got the first interview. She submitted online with a hundred other applicants. Did I mention earlier the *wonderful* resume that I had written for her? It was worthless for this online posting. That *general resume* never would have taken her to the next round.

Without a resume tweaked and tailored for this specific position and a comprehensive CCL, Mary Kay would have received an automatic reply: "Thank you for submitting your resume. While you are quite accomplished, we decided to focus on candidates who have stronger management backgrounds and qualifications in our industry. We will definitely keep your resume on file for future opportunities." Yep, the circular file.

Never blast a generic resume out to multiple postings on job boards. "Honey, I have applied for twenty-three jobs on CareerBuilder today (by pushing "submit resume" twenty-three times). I'm exhausted. Can we have dinner now?" Are you guilty of this? Can't understand why you get the same result time after time?

You should also send CCLs to recruiters who have connected with you. By writing a positioning letter to the recruiters, they will have a better idea if you are the right fit for the jobs they are currently filling. You may now be on their roster of qualified candidates for future opportunities. The CCL can also be used to approach people within your *warm network*—people who may know you well but do not have the ability to sell you as well as you can sell yourself.

Michael, a client with an impressive background in IT architecture, had a close friend who worked for Amazon. His friend offered to circulate his resume among various Amazon hiring managers and also slip it through the back door (over the transom) of human resources. Michael revised his resume to include stories (TSNs) that were relevant to the company and added the certifications and skill sets that were required for multiple positions at Amazon. Before he submitted the polished resume to his childhood friend, I put the brakes on his plan.

"You've done an excellent job with your resume. You have customized it perfectly. I want you to do one more thing. Write a conversational cover letter to your friend and hand-deliver it with your resume."

"Why? I've known Kevin since the third grade. He can promote me better than anyone."

"Better than yourself? When Kevin circulates your resume, he will also circulate your cover letter, written in your own words, and that is the best way to sell yourself throughout Amazon. Kevin can't do that nearly as well as you."

"What do I say in the letter? It's like bragging about myself to my brother!"

"You can start the letter off with gratitude. 'Dear Kevin, Thank you for sharing my resume with your associates at Amazon. As you know, my background in IT architecture includes …' Then tell your story as if you were explaining your background to the director of HR. Encourage Kevin to attach the letter to your resume. You now have the ability to tell your story to all interested parties in your own voice, not Kevin's."

Michael followed my advice and secured a position at Amazon quickly, bypassing the standard online process. Wake up and smell the revised resume and conversational cover letter.

CHAPTER 9

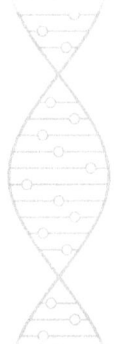

BUT WAIT, THERE'S MORE!
(YOUR SIXTY-SECOND COMMERCIAL)

Several years ago we had the bright idea of creating videos of our clients to share online. I instructed clients on how to write a sixty-second script (approximately one hundred words) with a structured beginning, middle, and end. The opening included a branding statement defining the level of the professional, the middle section communicated how the client does their job, and a powerful close expressed what the client could do for the employer's company.

This video was a verbal version of the profile. Clients rehearsed their scripts in front of mirrors so they could see how they appeared in their performances and with tape recorders so they could hear the energy and enthusiasm (or lack thereof) in their voices. We would set a cue card by the camera, and when the clients read their lines, it appeared as if they were speaking off the cuff and looking deep into the eyes of their audience.

It was a good marketing tool. The client could direct the potential employer to a link with a brief profile, a full resume, and a little video box (the size of a business card) that played the client's "commercial." The videos were pretty vanilla; the client was standing in front of a white wall, the sound was tinny, and their eyes were bouncing around like pinballs. The videos were in color, but they still had the appearance of a B movie, sans the 1940s film scratches. This was when LinkedIn was in its infancy, but the commercial, like LinkedIn, created an online presence for the client.

The novel idea started to take off, and we quickly improved the production value of the videos. We would open with upbeat music and an animated graphic with the client's name filling the screen. Fade in on the client, dressed to the nines and nestled in a stylish business office with a music bed humming along as she read from a teleprompter. As the client mentioned her skill sets, bullet points magically appeared over her shoulder, listing her impressive core competencies. Powerful closing statement, cut to animated graphic, music up and under, fade to black. There you had it—the sixty-second commercial.

These were quite popular—for a while. HR managers and C-Level execs loved the new concept. They could look beyond the paper resume and actually see personality and credibility. They were motived to meet the applicant for an interview. Then YouTube became popular. Everybody and his brother were creating "video resumes," and HR departments were inundated with moving pictures and online links. The fad faded quickly. There were actually lawsuits filed against companies in which applicants claimed that they were rejected due to their videos: "You don't like the color of my tie, my skin, my age …" This is when we pulled the plug on the monster we had created.

I always learn something new from all (or most) of my clients. I learned a valuable lesson when we patiently produced all of these commercials. Most clients were a little clumsy in front of the camera. Some would pull a "Cindy Brady" and stare at the lens speechless, with a glazed look in their eyes. Their only goal was to get through this agonizing video without stammering, stumbling, or embarrassing themselves. We would never put a commercial online that was less than flattering for the client, and we produced hundreds of these fireside chats. What did I learn from this? When you have a goal of successfully moving from point A (the opening of the commercial) and reaching point B (the close), everything in between is incidental.

The client had already organized their thoughts and written them in a script. We edited the script, and they became familiar with the structured beginning (branding statement), middle (accomplishments), and end (power close), which were all customized for the job opportunity. Irrespective of the video presentation, they had mastered the format and delivery of an opening statement that could be used at the start of any interview.

We call this the TMAY – **Tell Me About Yourself**. This is the first request in any interview where the applicant has an opportunity to brand themselves, deliver skill sets and achievements, and create an agenda of points they can refer back to throughout the ensuing interview. Most job applicants fail to take advantage of this perfect opportunity to make a great first impression. Out of nervousness, they may talk excessively and reveal superfluous or, worse, personal information:

Interviewer: Tell me about yourself.

Applicant: Well, I'm well organized and detail oriented, and I manage others with patience and compassion. I like long walks on the beach, pretty sunsets, and golden retrievers. My grandbabies mean the world to me...

Interviewer: Thank you. We'll get back to you. Next!

When one of my clients delivers their TMAY, the interviewer's jaw usually drops. That's a good thing. The interviewer is delighted to hear a structured statement that is personalized to the company and the position. The applicant has immediately established a rapport and created an agenda of what they will discuss throughout the interview. They have taken control in the first minute of conversation. The applicant can now expand on the skills and talents that they advertised in their opening statement and can easily refer back to the accomplishments that they strategically inserted in their TMAY.

I have clients start with a script written for a video presentation. The content is structured and organized and includes a power close. It is important to have a definitive close—wrap up the TMAY with what you can offer the organization. Most applicants end their opening statements with selfish pitches: "I am seeking an upper-management position in operations where I can grow within the company and take the organization to greater heights." But it is better to close with what you can bring to the company, not what you want for yourself: "With my PMP certification, expertise in lean manufacturing, and application of Six Sigma principles, I will increase productivity and profits for a progressive organization."

I then have the client read the commercial to me word for word. They sound scripted, awkward and over-rehearsed:

> Hello, my name is Christine Nicholson. I am a dynamic, self-motivated leader with over fifteen years of executive management experience in new business development and operations.
>
> I lead by mentoring, directing, teaching, coaching, and motivating my team to offer their own unique skills and talents. I have a proven track record of analyzing and defining problems in tough and austere environments, and then creating innovative solutions that break the cycle of failure and propel the company to success.
>
> I believe in aligning my clients' intentions and plans with their actions and words to help achieve their overall goals. I provide a service that sets my clients apart from their competition by focusing on the things that set them apart as quality providers of goods and services. Together, we change the way their customers act by changing the way they think.

After the client has read the script out loud, we discuss performance. Was she confident and believable? How was her pacing and enunciation? Was she consistent with her energy and enthusiasm from beginning to end? I then have the client reduce the script to four bullet points:

- ❑ Opening (branding statement)
- ❑ What they do
- ❑ How they do it
- ❑ Power close

We then turn the script over, and the client presents their opening statement from the bullet points. This allows them to speak naturally, use their personality, and powerfully close their statement in under one minute. It's amazing to watch this transformation. The client speaks with confidence (rarely referring to their notes), looks into my eyes, and delivers the message with clarity and conviction.

Few job applicants open with clear and concise statements. When you are driving to the interview and organizing your thoughts for your TMAY, ask yourself the following questions: How am I branding myself for this position? What are the key components they are seeking for the perfect applicant? How can I close by showing them that I am qualified to fill this position?

Of course you won't have a note card as you present your TMAY. But if you know yourself as a professional and know how you can successfully accomplish the company's goals and objectives, you can deliver your TMAY credibly, anytime, anywhere.

CHAPTER 10

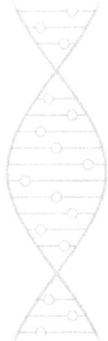

DOES THIS RESUME MAKE ME LOOK TOO FAT?
(THROWING YOUR HAT INTO THE RING)

How do you look—professionally? Before you apply online, you have to get your act together. Be sure to clean up your social media. Employers will look at your Facebook and Twitter accounts. When they Google your name, what will they see? Many companies pass on applicants because their colorful online presence does not fit into the company's culture. I believe in freedom of expression as much as the next guy, but you are now on display, inviting others to judge you, when you apply for a position. You should have an updated LinkedIn account with a professional photo. You should have a professional email address that does not include your birth year. Addresses like groovyguy1963@atl.com or love2partygirl@xyz.net are not going to earn points with hiring managers. Create a Gmail account with your name in the address.

Let's go through an example to illustrate several key points. You search an Internet job board and run across a position that looks like a match for you. Tailspin Aerospace has posted an opening for a "Project Manager / Engineer." You were laid off from Final Approach Aeronautics three months ago, and this posting appears to be similar to the position you held for fourteen years. You feel that this is the perfect fit, and you are tempted to apply immediately.

Slow down, chief; you're jumping the gun. Your first step is to copy the posting and glean the key requirements (the company's wish list) to enable you to compose your CCL and full resume, both of which will be customized for this position. You will then pull out of this job board and go directly to Tailspin's website to see if the position has been posted there. Well, what do you know? The exact same job description is residing in the "Tailspin Careers" section. This is where you will apply. Why go through two applicant-tracking systems and run the risk of being eliminated from the initial job board?

Now that you are on the company's site, gather intelligence. Learn as much as you can about the company: its mission statement, history, and principal players (decision makers). Information equals power. Your extensive knowledge of the organization is flattering to the employer, and an obvious lack of knowledge can be crippling and may disqualify you immediately. Send your cover letter to a key DM along with the HR director as a backup. You want to direct your letter to an actual person rather than opening with the generic salutation "To Whom It May Concern."

You identify Richard Burlingame as the vice president and director of engineering and decide to select him as your key contact. You now have an actual person to tell your story to in your conversational cover letter. Your next step is to go to LinkedIn and find out whether Tailspin Aerospace has a company page. They do! Now follow the company. Search for Richard Burlingame. There he is … not a bad-looking guy … looks nice enough. Hey, we went to the same school! Put out a request to connect with him. If Richard accepts your invitation, he will notice that you are following his company, the two of you share common connections, and you have the same alma mater. As he pours over the two hundred resumes that are about to hit his desk, maybe you will stand out. Top-of-mind awareness (TOMA)—it couldn't hurt.

It's time to write your CCL to Mr. Burlingame and tweak your resume. Afterward, merge the pages into one PDF or Word document (in case you are only allowed to upload one document online), and prepare the CCL and resume (both on resume paper) for mailing.

Before you go to the company's website to fill out the application, you need to have a good idea of the compensation range for this position in your market. If asked to specify a salary, you don't want to come in too low or too high.

You can search "free salary calculator" online. Never pay a fee for this public information. You will usually be asked three questions:

Q: What is the position?
A: Project manager / engineer

Q: What is the industry?
A: Aerospace

Q: What is the market?
A: Tucson, Arizona

You complete the questions on your chosen website, and the results page appears. At this particular website (not all results pages look similar), you see three or more manager/engineer levels listed on your screen:

- Level one salary range: $40,000–$53,000
  (This level requires the least experience and education.)

- Level two salary range: $50,000–$65,000
  (This level requires a bachelor's degree, five years of experience, and more job responsibilities.)

- Level three salary range: $70,000–$85,000
  (This level requires a bachelor's degree, master's preferred, PMP certification, and additional job responsibilities.)

You are surprised that $85,000 is the top salary being paid for this position in Tucson. When you held this job in Pittsburg, you were making $105,000. Well, that was several years ago, and this is Tucson, after all. I guess you have to pay for the sun and the sand. You were earning $76,000 at Final Approach Aeronautics before the company laid you off.

What salary would be too low for you? You need to establish your acceptable salary range and create a "walk away" number in your mind. With your skills, education, and experience, you will show the company where you can add value and hopefully break the $85,000 barrier, but you'd like to make at least $79,000. Now, this is a number that you do not share with anyone—not even the family dog (you don't know who Sophie talks to). If the company offers $68,000, you need to be prepared to show that the job requires $79,000 plus in experience, education, and credentials.

You are now prepared to tackle the online application. One of the first inquiries may be, "What are your salary requirements?"

You enter "open" and you get an instant alert: "Must enter a numeric value." While this puts you at an immediate disadvantage, at least you did your homework and have established the documented salary range for this particular market. If the position described is clearly level three, you should enter the median figure, if the salary calculator provides it; otherwise you can enter any value within the stated range—for example, $80,000. If you had entered the salary you earned in Pittsburg, $105,000, you would have priced yourself out of the market. If you are invited for a face-to-face interview, you will be able to justify the $80,000 figure and show where your education, experience, and expertise can add value, and perhaps you can move this number to $85,000 or beyond.

You have researched the company thoroughly and, more importantly, effectively communicated in your CCL how you fit within the company. As you are asked questions during the online application process, refer back to your notes in order to validate your qualifications. If you are only allowed to upload your resume, use the merged document that you previously prepared (which includes the CCL and resume) and beam it aboard. Now when the document is scanned, all of your key words and phrases will register.

After you have submitted online, mail the documents to Mr. Burlingame directly. After a few days, make the call to ask whether Mr. Burlingame received your correspondence. You may get the same response as Mary Kay received (in the previous chapter), but the call gives you the opportunity to see where the company may be in the interviewing process and make that third impression.

CHAPTER 11

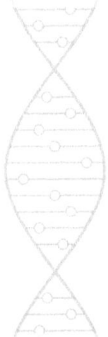

THERE'S NO BUSINESS LIKE SHOW BUSINESS!

The thing you gotta know is everything is show biz.
—Mel Brooks

Interviews are performances, and performances must be practiced. You must be prepared to answer tough interview questions. Have you prepped properly? What is your TMAY? What questions have you anticipated, and how are you prepared to answer them?

Have your top TSNs primed and ready. It is always best to include an accomplishment in each response whenever possible. It's one thing to tell me you can ride a horse; it's better to show me *how* by backing your answer with a SAR illustrating how accomplished you are as an equestrian. You should never try to be something that you are not; the interviewer will see right through you. Be yourself, answering the questions truthfully while qualifying your answers. Your performance should be brimming with a positive attitude, energy, and enthusiasm, and most importantly you should know your audience.

As you sit with others in the lobby, sizing up your competition, you may notice an applicant who was on your son's Little League team. Does the song "Life's Run Over My Face a Couple of Times" go through your mind? Competition is fierce these days, and the applicant pool is full of younger faces with fresh degrees who are willing to work for much less money.

Many companies overlook more experienced (older) applicants and hire more agile (younger) candidates in order to save money. As an employer, I take the opposite approach. Our company embraces age—in most cases, age equals experience. A seasoned, experienced employee has faced and overcome challenges and arrives at the table better prepared. If you fall into this category, you need to effectively communicate the professional accomplishments that most qualify you for the position.

Let's look at some difficult questions that you might be asked during an interview and consider some possible responses.

How do you deal with an underperforming employee?

A good response:

I like to see if the employee can explain what the company expects of them in their role. I have to see whether they understand the basic functions of the job before I can identify the actual problem. Once we've identified the problem, I work with them until they improve their performance. I believe in recognizing an individual's strengths and mentoring them to reach our desired goal.

The wrong way to answer would be to bring up disciplinary action or dismissal. Writing up or firing an employee is quick and easy. The applicant who brings this up shows their negative side. Remember, you must remain positive with all of your answers.

How do you perform under stress?

The wrong answer:

I thrive under stress. I work under stressful conditions daily, and I perform at my best when stress is in the air.

What you do not know about this question is that, to an HR director, *stress* is a four-letter word. I know, when I used my fingers to count, I also came up with six letters—but you must understand that this is a trick question. Stress is a signal that things are beyond one's control. It's a cop out (as we used to say back in the day); it's used as a crutch or an excuse. It is important to respond without using the word *stress* in your answer; gently redefine "stress" using another word.

Here is something else you may have missed: any "how" question anticipates a response that includes a formula, recipe, or breakdown of *how* you actually handle certain situations. When you are asked a "how" question, don't answer, "Quite well." That's what the magician says after you ask, "How did you do that trick?" You need to provide a detailed answer. Don't just say it—show it.

This is the right answer:

Our business faces unexpected challenges on a regular basis. When I am suddenly dealing with a challenge, I assess the problem, analyze options, collaborate with my team to discuss possible solutions, and act to implement the solution.

Problem or *challenge* are better words to use when redefining stress. We can control unexpected problems and challenges. Remember, when responding to a "how" question, you must present a step-by-step explanation showing how. This is an excellent opportunity to support your answer with a measurable accomplishment. Keep it brief, using the SAR framework: situation, action, result.

Do you think you will have any difficulties in transitioning from your current industry into our widget industry?

Avoid giving a poor answer like this:

No. I can learn the ins and outs of the widget industry, and in time I know that I would be a good performer.

The interviewers most likely feel that there is a lot to learn about their industry, and you are coming in cold. This is an excellent opportunity to use a SAR to show them how you faced change in the past and quickly came up to speed.

Here is a complete response:

I recognize the transition and understand there will be a learning curve. I have experienced industry and process change in the past. A good example is when I was with Taylor Manufacturing. As the program manager for the bicornic sleeve, we were expected to change our quality-assurance program to reduce the number of failed parts to 3 percent within three months. Applying Six Sigma principles and lean-manufacturing methodology, I oversaw the process change, and we lowered the failure rate to 1 percent in thirty days, under time and under budget.

Show that you have successfully faced transition in a short timeline. The employer is concerned that several months will pass before you can learn to do your job efficiently. You need to demonstrate that you learn quickly and will hit the ground running.

Do you think that you are overqualified for this position?

If you are doing a wonderful job in the interview, showing how your skills and experience perfectly match this position, good for you. However, let's imagine that I have a midsize company and I am very impressed with your ability. I may be concerned that I can't afford you, you appear to be very ambitious, and you will want to quickly graduate to the next higher position in the company—my job, which I don't want to give up.

You appear to be quite accomplished; you've done it all and done it successfully. I fear that you will get bored with this position and will jump ship with the first opportunity that comes your way. All of these things may be left unsaid on my part, but they drive me to ask this question: You have successfully worked at larger companies and in positions that held greater responsibilities; do you think that you are overqualified for this position with my group?

Wrong path:

> I may be overqualified for this position, but I really enjoy working in this role, and I feel that I can do an excellent job and make a valuable contribution.

You've just shot yourself in the foot. The interviewer has already come to the conclusion that you are overqualified and doesn't want to invest in a candidate who will lose interest quickly and take the next golden opportunity, possibly with his competition. You have just confirmed the interviewer's greatest fear.

A better response:

I would have to say no. With my education and experience, I believe that I can help the company grow. I am familiar with many of the problems that your company may encounter, and with my experience I can solve the problems quickly. I am motivated by unexpected challenges and have the ability to navigate the organization to a successful solution. I would have to say that with my proven history of problem resolution, I am quite ***prepared***.

Prepared is the magic word. When you show that you know where the rocks are in the road, your many years of experience will be embraced, and your age is now an asset.

Are you willing to relocate?

An incorrect response:

Well, maybe … we are a little upside down on our mortgage. We're looking after my eighty-two-year-old mother, and little Margie is in her sophomore year at Edison High.

By answering this question in any way other than the affirmative, you have just disqualified yourself from the job. The company may want to move you to Denver in nine months, and you just ended the interview. This question is asked at the beginning of the interview to qualify you for a possible move.

The correct response is short and simple:

Depending on the opportunity, I would certainly consider relocating.

I don't care whether you're wearing an ankle bracelet, and the sheriff won't let you leave the county. I'm sure there is a way to arrange a work-release program. If you don't answer (without the slightest hesitation) in a positive way, you will automatically be eliminated. The employer will disclose a possible relocation when they extend the offer. You can always graciously decline—but you need to get to the offer.

And now, the Big Kahuna of ridiculous questions:

What's your greatest weakness?

Please don't say, "Chocolate." Please don't eagerly offer a weakness that will earn you a half point for answering honestly but ultimately cost you the job. When you fall into this trap by providing a weakness, you are negatively branding yourself and will (if hired) forever be known as "that guy" or "that gal" who lacks patience, computer skills, communication skills, the ability to manage anger or handle stress—whatever.

How could a quick admission in response to this question possibly help you? You should never lie or withhold information. But this is a trick question, and casting a spotlight on any weakness cannot help you in any way.

There is a better way to honestly answer this question:

> I can't think of any weaknesses that would apply to this position. If any were pointed out to me, I would do my best to overcome them immediately. Let me give you an example. Earlier in my career, as a younger manager, I was given my first project to manage. I'm a bit of a perfectionist (and I think that's an asset), and I wanted to take on the entire project on my own. Fortunately, a senior-level manager observed this and took me aside. He told me, in not-so-kind words, that I had a very talented team to work with—many of them were more talented than me. This was my opportunity to draw from this pool of knowledge, collaborate, and lead the team. I followed his advice. The project was far more successful than it could have been if I had controlled it on my own. That was the day that I became a project manager and a leader. I have been leading others in a collaborative environment ever since.

What was accomplished here? First and foremost, you did not admit to a *current* weakness for *this* position. You did, however, provide a situation where you disclosed a professional limitation—but you buried it in the past and showed how you overcame the weakness. There is no doubt that you are not bringing this weakness to the table if you're hired for the position. Certainly the interviewer can recall personal weaknesses that they have overcome, and this actually bonds the two of you professionally. Great managers are not born; they evolve into leaders.

Here is another good response:

> Earlier in my career, I was petrified to speak in public. I used to stutter as a child. I could communicate one-on-one, but if there were more than two people in the room, I would freeze up. I once drove around the Citibank building three times and went up and down the elevator twice before I could walk into a conference room and give a simple five-minute presentation. I knew I had to overcome this problem if I were to move forward in my career. I practiced at night, reading scripts into a tape recorder in front of a mirror and my dog until the dog lost interest and left the room. I took Dale Carnegie courses and spoke in front of strangers at seven in the morning at a local Denny's for my Toastmasters group.
>
> Finally, I became less self-conscious, and I could speak naturally without stammering. I volunteered for speaking engagements with my company. I became the face and voice of the organization with the media. You may have seen me on the six o'clock news last night when our chemical plant was burning to the ground; I was calmly assuring a group of hostile protesters that no toxic chemicals were being released into the atmosphere. I'm proud to say that I will be the keynote speaker at the Global Widget Summit in Glasgow this summer.

Okay, that's a little over the top, but you get the point. The secret is simple: define a personal weakness, put it in your past ("earlier in my career"), and show how you moved beyond the problem.

Similar to the "greatest weakness" question is the line, "Tell me about three of your greatest professional failures." Interviewers love to work in threes, but providing three examples will not help you in any way. You need to regain control of the interview at this point.

I recommend that you look your interviewers squarely in the eye and reply, "I cannot recall three professional failures. I can discuss one situation that could have potentially led to failure." Then bring up a past occurrence that could have led to a catastrophic outcome had you not intervened and saved the company from failure. This is an application of the "greatest weakness" save. You discuss a problem (in the distant past) that you recognized and resolved.

Out of fairness and kindness, they may ask, "Tell me about three of your greatest professional successes." Now you can respond with three examples. You have a warehouse full of SARs that you can easily share. Just be sure that you offer success stories that are relevant to this company, industry, and position.

There are a number of screening questions designed for negative responses. Your strongest offense is to open with a powerful TMAY and answer questions with positive responses. Always support your answers with SARs showing where you can add value to the organization. You should have a list of questions that you will ask the interviewer at the end of the meeting. Many of these questions will come to mind during the interview, topics you wish to clarify. Here are two powerful questions that should always be asked by the applicant: "What are some of the immediate objectives for the company?" and "How does this position play a part in achieving these goals?"

This is a nice way of saying "Where have you failed in accomplishing your goals, and what do you need to achieve success?" without pointing a finger to the last person who held this position. You now have the opportunity to assure the employer that, with the application of your skills and experience, you can take the organization to the next level. This is where you prove that you can add value over and above the basic job requirements. I doubt that your competition is doing this.

Your last question should be: "What is our next step?"

After the first interview, whether it was over the phone or face-to-face, you must write a thank-you letter. You make a better impression if the letter is written in a professional format on resume paper and sent via US Mail. I know it is quicker and easier to send an email, but try to resist this trite temptation. Emails are disposable, forgettable, and many times they are never opened. A regular letter packs a powerful impression and will most likely be retained in your file. There may be a tight timeline; perhaps the company is going to make a decision within twenty-four hours, and you don't feel comfortable relying on the Pony Express. In this case, you should send an email *and* a hard copy of your letter. You can write a simple message in the body of your email:

> Dear Mr. Malone,
>
> I enjoyed meeting with you and Joan today to discuss opportunities with Valor.
>
> Thank you again for your time and consideration. I look forward to our next step in the process.
>
> Best regards,
> Annalisa Kane
>
> Attachment

Attach the letter you will be mailing to the email. When the attachment is opened, it will appear in the same format as the letter that will soon be delivered:

ANNALISA KANE
415-555-0237

www.linkedin.com/annakane　　　　　　　　　　　　　　　　annalisakane@gmail.com

November 19, 2016

Mr. Robert Malone
President
Valor Healthcare
4010 S. Atlanta Place, Suite 321
Dallas, Texas 75261-1661

Dear Mr. Malone,

I would like to take this opportunity to thank both you and Joan Newman for meeting with me to discuss the Controller position with Valor Healthcare. The professional atmosphere you presented was refreshing, and your enthusiasm for the organization was quite evident.

I want to thank you for recognizing my technical skills in both trend analysis and bottom-line enhancement, as well as my people skills in managing staff. I enjoy a challenging position that allows me to use my skills as a seasoned financial manager to make a valuable contribution.

I am very interested in becoming a member of the Valor team. If I can provide you with any further information, please do not hesitate to contact me. Thank you again for your time and consideration. I look forward to hearing from you soon.

Sincerely,

Annalisa Kane

You'll notice in the second paragraph that Annalisa reminded him of her skills that were recognized in the interview. Mr. Malone may have interviewed eight candidates, and her reference immediately puts her at the top of his mind. She also closed with a call for action: "I look forward to hearing from you soon." This simple thank-you letter could speak volumes.

CHAPTER 12

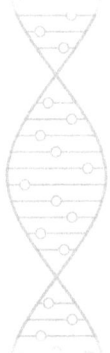

WELL PLAYED, SIR!
(NEGOTIATIONS)

Several years ago I met a friend for lunch at a local eatery, and he drove up in a brand-new dazzling convertible. The smile on his face nearly outshone the excessive chrome and fire-engine-red paint that swathed the hot ride as it glimmered and glistened in the Southwest sun.

"Congratulations! Your new car is beautiful!"

"Thanks! I don't know how Bashful Bob keeps his lights on. I got the deal of the century!"

Bashful Bob Automotive was the number-one car dealer in the county. Robert Morrison III (Bashful Bob) owned six dealerships that sold the most popular foreign and domestic automobiles of the day and was on local TV and radio airwaves around the clock. He was known for saying, "Go ahead, make me blush! I wanna sell *you* a car!" Bashful Bob was one of the most successful businessmen in the entire state, and his automotive empire employed over three hundred people.

"So, who sold you the car?" I asked.

"Gus Newberry, the general sales manager. He gave me his lowest fleet price."

"I know Gus. Isn't he their number one salesman?"

"Yep!" my friend said, beaming.

"Let's see, ol' Gus has been with Bob for about twenty years. He must stand on his feet ten hours a day and work six days a week."

"Yep." He smiled.

"How often do you buy a car?"

"Every four years, religiously …" The smile quickly faded from his face.

I didn't want to knock the wind out of my friend's sails, but you have to understand business. A good deal is only a good deal when it is a win-win situation. Bashful Bob would be delighted in knowing that my friend was spreading this story around town. This was free advertising through a wonderful testimonial. Bob made money; he'll keep the lights on.

I use this analogy with my clients when I'm assisting them in a negotiation. How often do you interview for a position and then hopefully negotiate your final deal? The company does this on a regular basis; they know how far they are willing to go even before the negotiation begins.

Most applicants don't realize that the negotiation begins in the first minute of the interview. As you sit down and deliver your TMAY, you are immediately taking control of the discussion and laying out an agenda for the duration of the interview. Throughout the interview you are showing where you can add value beyond the description of the job. You also have to be looking for holes on the company's side. What does that mean?

You are interviewing the employer as well. As you listen to the description of the job responsibilities, you need to ask yourself, what is being left out? You need to make a mental note of this and wait for a strategic time to bring up these missing items with the interviewer. Let's return to an earlier example to better explain this chess match.

Suppose that Richard Burlingame, the vice president of engineering, is interviewing me for the project manager / engineer position at Tailspin Aerospace. This is my second interview with the company; I have already graduated from the screening interview over the phone with the HR director. It is clear that I am qualified for the position, and Mr. Burlingame, whom I will now address as Richard, is about to put me through a behavioral interview, during which he will assess my technical ability, management style, and communication skills. I look good on paper, but he needs to see if I am a good fit for his team and blend well within the company culture.

I dodged the deadly "What do you need to earn?" question in the last meeting with HR. Money was never mentioned; the company must have been satisfied with the number that I provided in my application. Using an online salary calculator, I determined the salary range (for this market) to be $70,000 to $85,000 and specified $80,000 in my online application. The conversation begins like this:

Richard: John, Stacy was very impressed with you in her initial interview. The company has left it to me to discuss this position with you in greater depth and see whether you will be a good addition to my team. What are your salary requirements? What's it going to take for you to join the Tailspin family?

John: It's difficult to answer that at this point, Richard. I would like to discuss the position further and have a clearer understanding of my role on your team. Once we define the job responsibilities, I can tell you what I understand the compensation to be in this market based on my research. Let's discuss the position further, and then I'll be able to give you an intelligent answer.

This reply usually makes sense to the interviewer. I'm using logic: how can you expect me to tell you what I should be paid when I don't know what you want me to do for you? If Richard insists that I provide an answer before moving on, I can fall back on the number that was given in my application:

John: If you need an answer before we discuss the specific responsibilities in this role, with what I currently know about the position, it is in the $80,000 range. It could be more; it could be less. Let's discuss the job further, and I then I'll be able to provide an accurate number.

His next question may be, "What were you making in your last three positions?" This is a very personal and unfair question. He is trying to create a yardstick to measure me by. If I were at a party and someone asked me what I earned or how much money I had in the bank, I'd walk away, deposit my drink on them, or ask, "Why is that important to you?" Any of those three options usually works. But this is a job interview, and I don't want to offend Richard, even though he just offended me. He couches the question this way:

Richard: In your application, I noticed that you did not provide information on your salary history. You wrote, "Always compensated fairly for the job responsibilities." What is your current salary?

John: I'm sure we both agree that my experience and education qualify me for this position. With what I currently know about this job, it's quite different than my responsibilities at Final Approach Aerospace, so I believe it's unfair to compare the two. I'd like to discuss this opportunity further, and then I can provide an accurate compensation figure.

He may push harder and require a different answer to his question. I don't want to upset him—he may be my boss next week. If he insists that I respond, I will then qualify my answer:

John: If that is important for your decision, I was making $76,000. My base salary has been $70,000 for the last three years. However, each year I have established performance goals, exceeded my target and, received a $6,000 annual bonus. I earned my MBA two years ago, and I feel that I'm not being recognized for the additional skills that I am now offering the company. That is why I am very interested in this opportunity.

Satisfied with my answer, Richard moves into the interview. He asks several behavioral questions testing my technical aptitude and management style. He quizzes me with hypothetical workplace scenarios and listens closely to my answers and how readily I respond. Whenever it is appropriate to support my answer with a TSN, I jump at the opportunity. He is impressed that I have so many success stories that show I have proven ability in his field, and he is surprised at the ease with which I deliver the information.

We have now arrived at the turning point of the interview. Richard asks whether I have any questions for him. This tells me that he has completed his description of the job and its responsibilities and has concluded his interrogation. He has drawn the line and silently communicated that his part of this interview is now over.

Remember those holes I was looking for? I noticed that Richard never brought up the preparation and filing of compliance and regulatory forms, which must be submitted to the government on a monthly basis. He must have someone else doing that for him at additional time and expense. When I worked with Final Approach Aerospace, I labored over these reports monthly. I can now ask him who is taking care of this important task. He tells me that the company's legal department files the monthly reports. I tell Richard that I have been preparing these reports for years. It was an important part of my job at Final Approach, and I can easily handle this task for his company. I call this tactic the "coffee cup and coaster," patent pending, © 2013.

The coaster symbolizes Richard's description of the job from A to Z. Richard has a predetermined amount, X, of compensation that he is willing to pay me for every job responsibility that he just described—that's the empty coaster. The coffee cup (which is half full) represents the additional value that I can provide beyond the coaster. Had I prematurely mentioned the added value, Richard would have placed the coffee cup atop the coaster and said, "Sure, John, we expect you to handle the compliance forms," and then he would have paid me the predetermined X dollars. By separating the fundamental job description from the added value, I have asserted that I should be compensated for additional work and responsibility.

To better illustrate this, I can share the story of Lisa, a client interviewing for the director position at a small nonprofit organization. Lisa looked like she was sent straight from central casting to play the leading role for this highly regarded children's crisis center. Sophisticated and full of confidence, Lisa was also kindhearted, compassionate, and maternal, making her the perfect candidate to take this organization to the next level. The salary range of $60,000–$70,000 had been published on the organization's website, and after three interviews it was clear to Lisa that the organization was going to offer the full $70,000 with benefits. Lisa had done an outstanding job interviewing with all of the organization's board members. During the interviews, the board had shared their annual budget, showing her every expense and revenue stream.

As we prepared for her final negotiation, Lisa told me that year after year the organization budgeted $10,000 for a contracted grant writer. She expressed that the contract expense could be eliminated immediately because she was an experienced grant writer and could easily handle this responsibility. Lisa's grant writing experience had been noted in her resume, but the topic of grant writing had not come up during any of the interviews. The board probably assumed that expense was covered in the annual budget. Lisa strategically held back on any discussion of the topic so she could use the added value (coffee cup) as leverage in the final negotiation.

I asked her to estimate a conservative figure for her time and effort to write the grants. She quickly answered, "No more than $6,000. Who could be more knowledgeable than the director to write the grant? I've written grants for millions of dollars and 90 percent of them have been funded in full."

I advised her to bring copies of three of her most successful (fully funded) grants to review with the board during the final negotiation. I recommended that she place the value of her grant writing service at $7,000. This would create a win-win scenario. If they added $7,000 to her salary, they would have an additional $3,000 to dedicate to other areas that needed a budgetary boost. Lisa agreed and confidently prepared to close the deal. The next day she waltzed into my office, grinning from ear to ear. Now before I reveal what happened, I must tell you that my clients don't always follow my advice word for word.

"Please don't be mad at me, but I asked for the entire $10,000. You have to understand how impressed they were when I presented those grant proposals. I suggested moving the entire grant writing budget to my compensation package, and they didn't blink an eye. We agreed on a salary of $80,000, and I start next week!"

Well, I couldn't fault her for following her instincts. If they had rejected her number, they still would have negotiated to $6,000 or $7,000. In the eleventh hour of the negotiation, Lisa leveraged a valuable asset to enhance the predefined job responsibilities. The moral of this tale: Do not discount or give away the additional value that you can bring to an organization. Only disclose additional value-added job responsibilities during the final negotiation; otherwise, your treasured talents will be absorbed in the original job description—the coaster.

CHAPTER 13

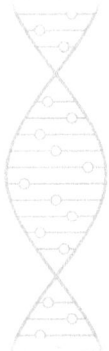

THE ART OF THE SPIEL

Incidentally, the proper Eastern European pronunciation is "schhhhh-piel." Now that we've cleared that up, on with our negotiation. I have just shown Richard the additional value I can bring to the organization, and he now hits me with his earlier question:

> **Richard:** Those are very good observations, John. I think you now have a complete understanding of this position. So tell me, what are you looking for in this role? What is a fair salary that you would be comfortable with?

I can now easily answer this question based on my research. Richard described a level-three position to me word for word. He never drifted from the language in the job posting or the information that I garnered from the online salary calculator. (Remember, the online calculator reported that the published salary range for a level-three position is $70,000–$85,000.) Though I had mentioned $80,000 earlier, throughout this interview I have clearly shown that I am an $85,000-plus professional:

> **John:** Well, Richard, you have clearly defined this as an upper level-three position.
>
> **Richard:** Level three?

I know he knows what "level three" is—he copied the description in his job posting from an online salary calculator.

> **John:** According to my research, a level-three position requires a bachelor's degree. I have my bachelor's and master's degrees in engineering, and I have just secured my MBA. This project manager

would assume the responsibilities you gave in the job description and must have ten years of industry experience. I have over sixteen.

Richard: Yep. What do you think that should pay?

John: The compensation for a level-three position in this market is upwards of $85,000.

The phrasing "upwards of" is critical. Richard and I both know the published range for this market is $70,000 to $85,000. I'm not going to let him cling to the bottom rung of the ladder ($70,000); this is not a car deal, and we aren't going to split the difference. If I've done my job right during this interview, I've shown him that I'm an $85,000-plus guy. By saying "upwards of," I've stated fact. At this point I feel that the ball is in the interviewer's court. If I do receive an offer, I've designed a strategy to negotiate a higher salary using the additional areas of expertise that I can bring to the position.

Richard hands me off to another VP who takes me on a tour of the facility and introduces me to various team members. As I return to the conference room, Richard is waiting with his assistant and asks me to take a seat:

Richard: John, I've chatted with upper management, and we'd like to make you an offer. We are quite impressed with your background, particularly your experience in lean manufacturing.

That's wonderful—I thought Richard was the final decision maker. By bringing in "upper management," Richard has introduced a "boss" who can negotiate any of my countering points.

John: Thank you, Richard.

Richard: We would like to bring you in as a senior-level engineer, which includes our platinum, five-star, golden, diamond-studded benefits package.

Hmm. Pretty name, but I have no idea what this sparkly package consists of. Richard is about to deliver a "good-news sandwich." The first slice of bread is the good news. I'm waiting now for the meat of this deal, which may be bad news.

John: Thank you.

Richard: For your first-year salary, we would like to offer you $78,257.

Where did that number come from? Employers in the nonprofit sector frequently back their offers down mathematically so they can award 3 percent raises each year and reach the high end of the posted salary range within three years. This job is not within that industry. Did I hear quarters bouncing off the conference table when I was walking back into the room? Were Richard and his assistant checking behind the sofa cushions for extra change to add to my offer?

There is one second that passes before I respond to Richard's offer. Let me tell you what is going through my mind during this one second of time:

1. Richard wants the best (that's me) for the least amount of money ($78,257).
2. Maybe some money can be made from the "golden" benefits package. I have to see it first.
3. My career coach has told me that I never, never, never accept or decline an offer on the day that it is extended. I need time to review and counter, so Richard is not going to get his answer today.
4. Richard's offer is very close to my walk-away number ($79,000), which I established in my mind in the event that I were offered a lowball figure ($68,000) so it is too close to matter.
5. Considering the published range of $70,000–$85,000, Richard's offer is closer to the high end, so I believe he is recognizing my senior-level ability.
6. One last thought—he offered me the job! He's interviewed several candidates, and he is serious enough to offer the position to me.

The second of time has passed, and I now react:

John: Thank you, Richard! I would love to be a part of your team. I believe we are close on the salary for the position that you described to me. If you would like for me to assume the various additional responsibilities that we discussed earlier, I'd be happy to do so, but of course the salary would need to be commensurate with the responsibilities. I would like to have an opportunity to review the benefits package.

Richard: Sure, John. I will email that to you.

John: Thank you. Could you email that with your offer and include the detailed job description? I'd also like a few days to review this and discuss it with my family. Can I get back to you by the close of business on Thursday?

Richard: Sure! I'll get the paperwork to you by the end of the day.

We shake hands and part ways.

Asking for a written offer was a very important move on my part. You must have the offer and all of the terms in writing; you cannot amend or sign off on a verbal offer. When an offer is not reduced to writing, the company can add responsibilities and conditions after you have started the position, and you won't have a leg to stand on when you complain to HR that you are doing the job of three people.

I go home, and within an hour I have an email from Richard. When I open it, I see the job description (from the original Internet posting) pasted within the content of a boilerplate contract. The benefits package is attached, and my eye is immediately drawn to the salary figure: $80,000. Is Richard playing mind games with me, or has he shown that he has made an effort to raise the figure to the highest number his company can offer? I'm not sure, but the salary will definitely be negotiated in the next meeting of the minds.

I study the "golden" benefits package. Not too shabby. The health benefits are much better than my previous company's package, and there is actually less out-of-pocket monthly expense. There's one catch: benefits don't start until ninety days after employment begins.

Let's imagine that I was actually downsized (laid off) from my previous company, and I am now enrolled in COBRA coverage. I have six people in my family, and the $1,000 monthly premium is killing me. It is now time to choose my battles. My first topic of negotiation will be to start my company coverage immediately, and if there must be a probation period (thirty, sixty, or ninety days), I'd like for the company to cover my COBRA payment.

The company has an attractive 401(k) matching program and generous tuition reimbursement for additional education but only offers one week of paid vacation after a full year of employment. I've been working for over three decades, and I am accustomed to at least three weeks of vacation. That will be another point of negotiation.

What about performance bonuses? I would like to establish a performance goal to be met within the first year of employment: if I can make or save the company $900,000 in the first twelve months, I would like a bonus of some percentage of my salary and possibly a promotion. If I should miss that goal by a few thousand dollars, I get nothing. Of course I'll kick myself, but I'm sure the company will be quite happy when I eventually save or earn them a significant amount. That's a win-win scenario.

I need to write all this down and prepare a professional way to bring up these topics when I regroup with Richard. This is a chess game of sorts. When the fur starts to fly in the negotiation process, I may lose track of what is most important to me. Richard is far more astute with this process and knows how far his company will go to close this deal. I want to keep it professional and consider the best resolution for both parties; yet I can't leave too much on the table. My adamant determination will be respected, but I know that I must be flexible. That is why I prioritize my topics of negotiation. In this example, they are as follows:

1. Salary
2. Insurance
3. Vacation

The negotiation concludes amicably, and my contract includes the following:

1. The salary starts at $85,000, with a performance review in six months; if goals are met, I will receive a 5 percent raise.
2. The company will cover my COBRA payment for thirty days and then immediately initiate my benefits (a $1,000 savings).
3. I will receive two weeks of paid vacation with an additional five days of unpaid personal time off.
4. If I am laid off, my paid severance will be extended from their standard two months to six months with full pay, health benefits, and outplacement services.

Every negotiation is different. There are many topics to consider, but you need to determine what is best for you. Does the company offer a signing bonus, stock options, or relocation reimbursement? Check on its policies regarding mileage reimbursement, travel expenses, and cell phone and computer expenses.

If you fail to recognize these benefits up front, you only have yourself to blame. If you try to bring these benefits up after you join the company, be prepared for a wrestling match. Negotiation is much like a courtship: it's easier to hash out the minutia before you enter into holy matrimony. Consider this your prenuptial agreement; work it out before you forge your partnership with the organization.

CHAPTER 14

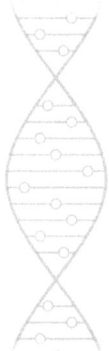

NETWORKING SAVES LIVES

When Randal walked into my office, I almost didn't recognize him. He was short of breath and lethargic, and his face was ashen. This man should be at home in bed.

"Sorry I missed our last meeting. I was in the hospital for a few days, and they think it may be my heart, but they haven't been able to completely diagnose my problem. They told me to take it slow and get some mild exercise. Today's meeting is my mild exercise. We need to catch up on our work."

I was speechless. Did he really expect me to conduct business as usual? Rethinking the situation, he uneasily asked if I might know of anyone who could give him a second opinion.

"Randal, I want you to call your wife to pick you up and take you home. You need to see a heart specialist. I'm going to make a call." I immediately called my good friend David Finer in Tulsa, Oklahoma. Books have been written about David. He is a cancer survivor, a philanthropist, a consummate businessman, an all-around great guy, and, most importantly, my dearest friend.

How could he help Randal? David is connected to numerous people from all walks of life, but he is most closely tied to the best of the best in the medical community. Friends jokingly refer to this as the "six degrees of Finer separation"—everyone is connected to this guy in some way. David comes to Tucson twice a year to have dinner with me and (since he happens to be in the neighborhood) undergo a series of tests to monitor his own heart problem. David is under the care of Dr. Mark Friedman, a renowned heart specialist who only sees David because they are good friends. In other words, Dr. Friedman does not take on new patients.

We had a problem here. Randal needed some answers quickly. He needed an expert, and I was going to do everything I could to make that happen. David took my call, and I explained the situation. I told him that my client was sitting in front of me, and we needed to get him into Mark's office as soon as possible. David told me to wait fifteen minutes for a call. For the next ten minutes, Randal and I stared at the phone and one another. The phone rang. It was Dr. Friedman's assistant. The doctor would meet Randal in one hour at the hospital.

Randal had emergency triple-bypass surgery the next morning. If he had done nothing (following the other doctor's advice), he could have unexpectedly left this world. A few weeks after the surgery, I had the pleasure of meeting Randal's wife and young son. I will never forget the look on this boy's face. There was a presence of maturity and compassion in his five-year-old eyes. He was wise beyond his years; he knew that he had almost lost his father and was very lucky to get him back. Six years later, Randal is living a healthy (medically monitored) life.

Thank you, David.

To me, this story is the epitome of networking. We don't know who our friends know. When you are looking for a job, you need to explore your warm network. The people you know are the path of least resistance to opportunity. When you approach a friend or associate and explain that you are exploring opportunities in a specific company or industry, they will usually lead you to a friend, acquaintance, or relative who can assist you. You are not asking them for a job; you are merely discussing opportunities and expanding your network.

While friends and associates are a good place to start, you need to create a network that includes professionals whom you do not currently know. When you are starting your job search, you must go beyond the Internet to find opportunity. The Internet is a black hole for job applicants. Thousands of people are scouring the same job sites as you and attaining the same lackluster results. We've discussed strategic tools to use when applying for posted positions. Use them, but don't totally rely upon them. Most positions are secured in the "unpublished" job market through people you know, or people *they* may know.

We call this a proactive (versus reactive) job search. Applying online to posted jobs is a reactive process. Your prospects are limited, and the playing field is overcrowded with competition. When you build a strong network of professionals who can refer you to others or create a position for you within their own companies, you are piloting a proactive approach that will unveil numerous opportunities. The competition is minimized, and you are in control.

Our clients conduct narrowly focused research on the companies, industries, and markets for which they are best suited. The Internet can reveal valuable information to the savvy investigator. Let's start with companies that you would like to work for. They may not have jobs currently posted on their websites, but they will be hiring at some point. Reach out to each company's upper-level management, specifically to decision makers (DMs) who are one or two levels above your desired position.

Target a DM and write an approach letter to secure a meeting:

JONATHON HUNTER
505-555-4606

www.linkedin.com/jonlhunter   jon.l.hunter@gmail.com

March 3, 2016

Mr. Aaron Diamond
Vice President
Northrop Grumman Corporation
100 Sun Ave. NE #300
Albuquerque, NM 87109

Dear Mr. Diamond,

I am researching various commercial industries in the Albuquerque area where my project management background might be applied, and I have come across Northrup Grumman as being a leader in the defense and research industry. It is because of your reputation and experience that I would like to have a brief meeting with you.

    Please understand that I do not expect you to know of specific opportunities at this time. However, I feel that I can benefit from your experience in the industry and trust that you can offer suggestions on how I might best utilize my skills. It is your advice and recommendations that will be most valuable to me. I am expanding my network in the Albuquerque area, and I'm anxious to see where my experience and skills can make the greatest impact in an organization.

    As a foundation for our discussion, I am enclosing a brief summary, highlighting my professional skills and experience. Appreciating that your time is valuable, I assure you that I will keep our meeting brief. I will call you in the next few days to arrange an appointment at your convenience.

Thank you in advance for your time and consideration.

Sincerely,

Jonathon Hunter

Attachment

Follow up by phone a few days after the contact has received the approach letter. The letter stated, "I will call you in the next few days to arrange an appointment at your convenience," so the recipient should be expecting the call.

A good rule of thumb is one week after the mail drop. Try to call mid-morning or midafternoon, Monday afternoon through Friday morning. Monday mornings are bad; people are clearing their desks to prepare for the week. Friday afternoons are challenging; people are trying to duck out of the office early to get a jump on the weekend.

When you make a follow-up call, your first obstacle may be the contact's gatekeeper. The gatekeeper's job is to keep you away from their boss. You want to be respectful—after all, the person answering the phone may actually be the DM (who just happened to answer the phone)—but you must also be firm and confident. If you show weakness or uncertainty, you will be eaten alive.

Remember, you researched this company and targeted a DM in the hopes of meeting and exchanging information about the industry and expanding your network. You wrote and rewrote a letter clearly stating your intention and invested in resume paper and postage—and you invested your time. You exhibited professionalism and should have every right to talk with your contact over the phone. Does that give you the confidence you need to handle a tough gatekeeper?

You need to anticipate three screening questions:

1. What company are you with?
2. What is this regarding?
3. Is he or she expecting your call?

You may be thrown with the "What company are you with?" question. You have confidently opened doors by using your company name in the past, but you don't want to use it here. You are working this on your own. The best response would be: "I'm not representing a company; I'm representing myself."

Let's imagine that I am following up on an approach letter that I sent to Bill Meyers, CEO of ABC Widgets. I addressed the letter to Mr. William R. Meyers, President/CEO. I am not going to open with "May I please speak with Mr. William Meyers?" That makes me sound like a bill collector. A more successful exchange would be this:

Gatekeeper: ABC Widgets, Bill Meyers' office, this is Sharon. May I help you?

John: Hi, Sharon. This is John Singer. I'm calling for Bill Meyers. Is he available?

Gatekeeper: John, what company are you with? What is this regarding?

John: I'm not representing a company, Sharon; I'm representing myself. I'm following up on some correspondence that I sent Bill last week. He's expecting my call. Is he available?

Bill may be jumping up and down in the doorway, frantically waving his arms, indicating that he wants to take the call, and Sharon motions him to calm down. Last month, she let the wrong person through, and Bill was pressured into buying three thousand talking key chains that sang his company jingle. Half of them were defective and started singing unexpectedly in customer's pants at the worst possible moments. She hasn't heard the end of this and is quite cautious about whom she sends through:

Gatekeeper: I'm sorry. Bill is not available. Would you like his voice mail?

John: Sure, Sharon, that will be fine. But please tell me—when is the best time to call Bill back?

By asking this, I'm letting her know that I am professionally persistent, and I want to make it easier on all of us by calling at a better time. I'm also letting her know that I am not going to give up and will probably call her every morning for the rest of her life. More often than not, she will take this cue and provide me with information:

> **Gatekeeper:** Well, he has an early meeting tomorrow morning, but he will probably be available around ten o'clock.
>
> **John:** Great, Sharon, I'll give him a call tomorrow at ten. I'll take his voice mail now. Enjoy the rest of your day.

This was a strategic move on my part. I have paved the way for my next call. I will call back tomorrow at ten o'clock sharp:

> **Gatekeeper:** ABC Widgets, Bill Meyers' office, this is Sharon. May I help you?
>
> **John:** Hi, Sharon. This is John Singer. You suggested that I get back with Bill today at ten. He's expecting my call. Is he available?

She'll send me through without the interrogation I endured yesterday. But what if Sharon is away, and Jessica answers Bill's phone? Here is how I would handle the conversation:

> **Jessica:** Bill Meyers' office, this is Jessica. May I help you?
>
> **John:** Hi, Jessica. This is John Singer. Sharon wanted me to get in touch with Bill today at ten. He's expecting my call. Is he available?

Jessica will put me right through without any questions. I mentioned Sharon's name, and I knew that Bill was free at ten—she has no reason to block my call.

Now, for my brief voice mail, I need to remember to do the following:

- Identify myself and reference my letter
- State that I want to meet with him
- Mention how and when I will get back to him

And it sounds like this:

Hi, Bill. This is John Singer. I'm calling to follow up on the letter that I sent you last week.

I'd like to arrange a time for us to meet. Sharon tells me that tomorrow at ten will be the best time to reach you, so I'll give you a call then. Thank you.

Some people may ignore these types of phone calls. They may have misinterpreted the purpose of the approach letter and sent the materials directly to HR. If you have left a few messages and the contact has not responded, a "second-attempt" letter may be in order:

JONATHON HUNTER
505-555-4606

www.linkedin.com/jonlhunter jon.l.hunter@gmail.com

March 21, 2016

Mr. Aaron Diamond
Vice President
Northrop Grumman Corporation
100 Sun Ave. NE #300
Albuquerque, NM 87109

Dear Mr. Diamond,

A few weeks ago, I mailed a letter to you introducing myself, and I also provided a brief career summary. I have called and left a few messages. Understanding busy schedules, we've missed one another. I am still very interested in talking to you about the defense industry here in Albuquerque.

My only purpose is to establish a network and discover where I can contribute my skills to an organization and make a significant impact. I do not expect you to know of any opportunities at this time, but given your background, I know that you could provide some great advice or possibly refer me to another manager in your organization to speak with.

I understand and appreciate the fact that you have a busy calendar, and hopefully you will be able to arrange some time for me to meet with you. I will give you another call to see if there is a time that will be convenient within your schedule.

Thank you for your time and consideration.

Sincerely,

Jonathon Hunter

"Understanding busy schedules, we've missed one another" is a very nice way of saying "You haven't had the decency to return my call, you self-absorbed son of a …" Maybe he was out of the office or doesn't think he can help you and hopes that you will eventually go away.

Ending the letter with: "I will give you another call to see if there is a time that will be convenient with your schedule" is a gentle reminder that you aren't going to disappear. But the most important content in a second-attempt letter is "I know that you could provide some great advice or possibly refer me to another manager in your organization to speak with." This allows the contact to pass the baton to another manager who may be more helpful.

A client once asked me, "Why would the head of an organization want to waste time meeting with someone like me just to discuss his company and the industry?" I told him that with *that* attitude, he didn't have to worry—no one would want to meet with him. (Tough love.)

Everyone you reach out to will not greet you with open arms. You have to confidently explain to them that you are expanding your network and that you do not expect them to know of specific opportunities. If they know that you are merely seeking an information exchange (professional to professional) and not sneaking past HR for a job, they will usually be happy to assist you.

There may be something in this for them. They could refer you to a friend or realize that in the future you may be an excellent addition to their team. If you've built a good rapport (made a new professional friend) and left with two or three referrals, you've been successful.

You must be totally prepared before you conduct this informational meeting. Research the contact and the company thoroughly. Connect with the contact and follow the company on LinkedIn. Have a solid TMAY that will brand your level of professionalism and exhibit skills and accomplishments that may be of value to the industry, not the company. Have five or more industry-related questions prepared. Anticipate questions that your contact may have for you.

After the meeting you will need to write a thank-you letter and send it immediately (via US Mail) while you are still on his mind:

JONATHON HUNTER
505-555-4606

www.linkedin.com/jonlhunter   jon.l.hunter@gmail.com

March 28, 2016

Mr. Aaron Diamond
Vice President
Northrop Grumman Corporation
100 Sun Ave. NE #300
Albuquerque, NM 87109

Dear Aaron,

Thank you so much for taking the time to speak with me today regarding my networking efforts and employment research. Your advice and recommendations were insightful and most appreciated.

    As you suggested, I will contact Rachel Hutchinson at Booz Allen Hamilton. Hopefully she will be able to provide additional insight and advice about the local business marketplace. I will also reach out to some of the other organizations that you referred to in the Albuquerque market.

    I look forward to expanding my network in the New Mexico area. Please let me know of any other individuals you believe could assist me in this regard. Again, thank you for your assistance, and I will be sure to keep you informed as to my progress.

Sincerely,

Jonathon Hunter

Create a spreadsheet to track those you've met with, what was discussed, and your next steps. You should follow up with these contacts periodically to keep them updated on your progress.

I have seen hundreds of clients build long-term relationships by applying this method. These relationships have led to jobs. Tables often turn; some of my clients have helped people whom they met through an information meeting secure positions years later.

You can and should be prepared to network with key professionals at industry events, at local gatherings, and during chance encounters. If you have a strong TMAY prepared for any opportunity, you'll be surprised how quickly your network will grow.

CHAPTER 15

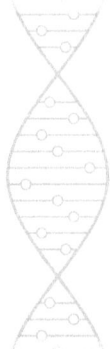

NEVER, NEVER, NEVER GIVE UP

On the corner of my desk, I prominently display a framed tile that reads:

> Never
> Never
> Never
> Give Up

This is one of my main mantras in life. The quotation is commonly attributed to Winston Churchill. These words have comfortably sustained and supported me through difficult times and elevated me to higher levels of productivity and happiness. Most of the clients that I work with are at the lowest points of their lives. They have lost their jobs, and many of them are in a state of desperation and depression.

Our company has the challenging responsibility of coaching and motivating clients to take the tools that we have provided, and move forward in their careers. We don't want them to settle for just feeding their families; we want to inspire them to feed their futures.

In a recent meeting, I was reviewing a client's job-search progress, and noticed that he was staring at the framed tile with a frustrated smirk on his face. "I've got to tell you, John—I'm on my third 'never.'"

Normally full of energy and optimism, Gerald had slipped into a "why me?" defeatist frame of mind.

He was waiting on an offer from a company that had assured him that a decision would be made by Thursday, but that was last Thursday. I advised him to ask himself, "Why *not* me? What am I going to do to change this situation?" He had not followed up as I had asked him to do last Thursday; he just waited by the phone for their call. Sometimes you have to show a little backbone, let the company know that you may have other options, and ask whether they are still interested in hiring you.

Gerald called the HR director from my phone. He told her that he had not heard from them as expected last Thursday and was calling to see where they were with their final decision. As it turned out, the final approval was to come from the CEO, and he had just returned to the office. She apologized and assured him that they would get back to him by the end of the day. Two hours later, Gerald received the offer.

I believe that if you've never quit, you've never failed. You will stay on the road to success if you are fully engaged in your career campaign and continuously ask yourself, "What else can I do? What should I be doing differently?"

Many, *many* years ago, I was just beginning my six-year struggle as a stand-up comedian in Los Angeles. Every Monday, the Westwood Comedy Store had an open-mic night. Young hopefuls waited in a long line to put their names on a list at 6:00 p.m. to secure a spot on stage that evening.

I had only been at this for a few months, and I was delighted to see I had secured a (prime) 10:00 time slot. As I paced in the parking lot at 9:30, going over my act, I noticed a long line of customers at the door. I entered through the back door and saw that the audience was completely full - standing room only. I was nervous and excited at the same time. I was about to go on stage in front of a packed house—this could be my big night! At 10:20, the emcee jumped on stage to introduce me: "Ladies and gentlemen, you seem like a good crowd, so we have a very special treat for you tonight. Please give a warm welcome for Robin Williams!"

Robin Williams weaved through the audience and jumped on stage. The room erupted with applause and cheers. I was shocked, hurt, and elated all at once. Robin was at the height of his career, and he often dropped by the Comedy Store to work out material for an upcoming concert or television appearance. He was quite simply a comedic genius, and I was in awe of him, as were my wannabe peers waiting in the wings. As he "killed" the audience over the next twenty minutes with his hysterical stream-of-consciousness banter, I suddenly realized that I was going to have to follow his amazing routine. After a forty-five-minute impromptu performance, Robin darted off the stage and exited through the front door, taking half of the autograph-seeking audience with him.

What was left of the room was abuzz and charged with energy. The emcee picked up the microphone and started to announce the next act. "Ladies and gentlemen, you've seen Johnny Carson, Merv Griffin, and *Saturday Night Live*. Well, our next comic has seen all of those shows, too! Put your hands together for John Singer!"

All of the voices in my head (and trust me, there were many) urged me to duck out the back door, hop into my battered '76 Cutlass S, and hightail it back to Oklahoma. But something made me stay. As I navigated my way through the empty tables, I heard a weak spattering of applause. I grabbed the mic, and with a big toothy grin, I yelled, "How you all doing?" Crickets. Nothing. Nada. You would have thought someone had just yelled "Fire!" in this once-crowded theater. Needless to say, I bombed horribly that night. Some say it was tantamount to Hiroshima.

Flash forward to five years later. I had slightly (ever so slightly) improved my act, and I was performing regularly. On occasion, I would emcee at Bud Friedman's Improv for their open-mic night on Sundays. One night Robin Williams snuck in the back to observe the young comics on stage. I asked him if he wanted to go on, and he smiled and shyly said that he just wanted to watch. I told him about the Comedy Store incident. He shrugged his shoulders with a silent "Sorry" expression. I told him that it made for a great story: "I tell everyone how Robin Williams opened for me."

There was an unusual comic on stage who called himself "Apple Butter." We were never sure about this guy; he dressed in overalls and a straw hat and in a dimwitted delivery told long stories about Washington Red Delicious apples. No one knew whether he was mentally challenged or a comic genius because on some nights he had the audience rolling in the aisles. This wasn't one of those nights; this audience did not understand his unique brand of humor. I asked Robin once again if he wanted to go on—I was going to take Apple Butter off the stage and save him from his misery. Robin immediately objected. He gave me that warm smile, and with a glint in his eye, he said,

"No, no, let him stay on. I love this guy. He never gives up! Neither did you."

For over six years, I performed in front of thousands of people—and actually entertained three or four, mostly family. One night, an audience member approached me after I left the stage and told me that he was an aspiring comic and wanted to talk about the business. After meeting for a cup of coffee, he told me that his sister had just moved to LA, and he wanted to introduce me to her. He set me up on a blind date, and after we fixed her eyes (sorry, it was just too easy), I married her. Thirty years later I think back to that night when this stranger (now my brother-in-law) approached me. I actually did not want to perform that night; I almost canceled. Had I not shown up for that chance encounter, five beautiful children would have never been born. Never give up; never stop trying.

I have had the honor of working with hundreds of professionals throughout the United States and internationally. My greatest reward is knowing that all of these people were inspired in some way, large or small, to apply these strategies and build successful career paths for the rest of their working days.

I hope that this book will help HR professionals identify qualified candidates and have a better understanding of their pools of applicants. I hope companies will see the advantage of offering outplacement services for their downsized employees and understand that such valuable care packages will quickly guide these employees to their next career opportunities. I mostly hope that the average reader will walk away with one or two good ideas that will help them soar professionally.

If any one of these hopes is realized, this handbook of professional-development strategies was worth the effort. My next creative venture will be a steamy romantic novel or a screenplay for a comedic buddy movie that reveals dark, dysfunctional family secrets.

My father taught me the most important lessons that I know about business. A few of his many pearls of wisdom will never leave me:

- ❑ Surround yourself with people more talented than you.
- ❑ Success is measured by how you have inspired others.
- ❑ Do what you love, and happiness will follow.
- ❑ Never give up.
- ❑ Go out and make it happen.

One day he took me aside and made an observation that I hope was a compliment. He put his hand on my shoulder, and with a warm smile and his southern gentlemen's charm, he said:

"Son, you're the kind of guy that will succeed in spite of himself."

I hope I haven't let him down.

My parting advice to you:

Go out and make it happen ... now.

ABOUT THE AUTHOR

As a certified professional resume writer (CPRW) and a dedicated career coach and advisor, John Singer has mentored and motivated professionals to identify their unique skills and talents and transition into meaningful and rewarding careers. As president and owner of *Professional Development Strategies,* John is committed to equipping clients with the necessary tools to communicate their strengths, build and establish professional networks, and secure positions that will allow them to soar professionally.

Earlier in his career, John was an episodic television writer and member of the Writers Guild of America. With a noted career in the broadcasting industry as a station owner/operator and radio personality, John combines his experience in business, marketing, and communication to inspire others to reach their highest levels of professional performance.

John Singer resides in Tucson, Arizona, providing outplacement services for companies internationally. He is a motivational speaker who educates and entertains his audience with practical advice on business, branding, career search, and life.